W9-CXF-438

fic a   21300

Fleming, Jo
His Affair

Galien Township Library
Galien, Michigan

   1. Books may be kept two weeks and may be renewed once for the same period, except 7 day books and magazines.

   2. A fine is charged for each day a book is not returned according to the above rule. No book will be issued to any person incurring such a fine until it has been paid.

   3. All injuries to books beyond reasonable wear and all losses shall be made good to the satisfaction of the Librarian.

   4. Each borrower is held responsible for all books charged on his card and for all fines accruing on the same.

Galien Township Library
2 1300

His Affair

Jo Fleming

His Affair

M. EVANS AND COMPANY, INC.
New York, N.Y. 10017

M. Evans and Company titles are distributed in
the United States by the J. B. Lippincott Company,
East Washington Square, Philadelphia, Pa. 19105;
and in Canada by McClelland & Stewart Ltd.,
25 Hollinger Road, Toronto M4B 3G2, Ontario

LIBRARY OF CONGRESS CATALOGING IN PUBLICATION DATA
Fleming, Jo.
His affair.
1. Marriage.   2. Marriage counseling—Personal
narratives.   3. Adultery—Personal narratives.
I. Title.
HQ734.F57   301.42   76-15245
ISBN 0-87131-216-6

Copyright © 1976 by M. Evans and Company, Inc.
All rights reserved under International and
Pan-American Copyright Conventions

Design by Joel Schick

Manufactured in the United States of America

9 8 7 6 5 4 3 2 1

✎ FOREWORD

If anyone had asked me, ten years ago, if my marriage could be rocked by infidelity, I would have laughed indulgently at such a ridiculous question. I was sure that my husband and I loved each other more than any other couple I had ever known—and I was equally certain that we knew all the most appropriate and constructive ways of handling whatever problems arose, so that such a devastating and painful experience could not possibly occur.

Both of us had grown up in traditional, middle-class families. We were exceedingly naive about other people's lives. Neither of us believed, in principle, in adultery; we viewed it as a symptom of serious disturbance. Because we were in love and were psychologically sophisticated, we would never even get close to having to deal with such a problem.

The truth is that we *are* remarkably stable; people who know us well consider us extremely well adjusted. That is what makes me feel that our story may be helpful to others. There is no immunity from crisis and pain in the human experience. The only variable is what we do about it.

I wish it were possible to use my own name as author of this book. I am proud of it; I am proud of the life and the growing it describes. If it were my decision alone, there would be no problem. But many other people are involved, and too many would be profoundly shocked and hurt. It seems to me that the story ought to be able to stand on its own—that if it will mean anything to other people, it need not be at the expense of such unnecessary wounding.

Ending

◡◞ *FIRST DAY*

Nothing will ever be the same again.

Inside my head I am screaming, screaming, screaming. Dear God let me die; let this plane crash this second, give me oblivion. Please! Please! I can't stand the pain, I can't live, I want to die. Now, this minute.

My husband Jerry sits in the aisle seat across from me. We always take two aisle seats because he has such long legs. We have been married for twenty-six years. He is my best friend. But my teeth are chattering and I am screaming inside and falling apart because at this moment he is reading a letter. And I can see some of the words, without moving my head at all. The letter starts, "My Dearest Dear, Have missed you so much and will be so glad to see you." I know who the letter is from. I handed it to Jerry while we were checking out of the hotel just a couple of hours ago. While he was paying the bill, I went to check the mail. Just this one letter for him. "N. Goodman" in the upper left-hand corner. A slight sense of uneasiness when I see it—a sudden dead agony in the pit of the stomach when he seems flustered that I hand it to him.

The trip to the airport was full of vague demons floating through space around my head. A sense of foreboding—doom. But also uncertainty. Nothing real. Busy-ness before we leave. Meeting some of Jerry's colleagues—heading for home. We explain needing two aisle seats and are relieved when we are given seats among strangers. It's been a long trip and so much talking.

The plane does not crash. It seems impossible that no one hears my internal shrieking, that Jerry doesn't notice I have already committed suicide inside my head. I go through all the motions of being alive. We talk, eat, smile, go to the john, wonder aloud about whether or not Julie, our twenty-one-year-old daughter, will meet us at the airport with her boyfriend, Andy. Jerry hates to be met, wants to just "get home with no fuss." I think that if they are there, I will become hysterical, start shouting and sobbing and running around like the maniac I know I have just become. They *can't* be there. No one could wish me more suffering than I am already experiencing—there must be some limit to the vengeance of the gods. Vengeance; yes, that's the word. It is my fault. I am getting old and ugly. I have taken Jerry for granted. We have just had a lousy vacation, snapping at each other, feeling tired and cranky. I have experienced moments of acute isolation followed by a nonspecific kind of rage I couldn't identify. I have become a nagging hag. He's sick and tired of me. And I don't want to live without him. I haven't got the guts to kill myself, so there is nothing to do but pray for mercy, pray to die.

Nina Goodman. She must be about thirty-five years old now. Ten years ago she had worked as an assistant under Jerry. UNDER! What else was she doing UNDER him? Did it start that long ago? Impossible. But so is now impossible. I remember Jerry used to tell me about her. She was a frail, uncertain girl, an immigrant from Europe, a brilliant student but lacking in self-confidence. She had been involved in a stormy love affair when she and Jerry began working together, and I remember Jerry had been her confidante and go-between. He had told me about their meetings—even to having spent time at her apartment when they were working together. That was about ten years ago, and once in a while he'd mention her or she'd call to speak to him. I wondered sometimes if she'd fallen in love with him, but we were so close, Jerry and I; we told each other everything. We had fought so hard for each other—nothing could come between such friends.

There is to be no mercy. The rack. There is beautiful, loving, smiling Julie, waiting at the gate. There is sweet, gentle Andy, wanting to carry our bags to his car. How lucky we are to be met by such loving young people. How I wish Julie were in Katmandu at this moment in my life! She bubbles on the way home. Did we have a good time? Did we go on any special sightseeing trips? Julie has made a special gourmet dinner for us, to welcome us home. It is now eight P.M., New York time; one in the morning by our inner clocks. I don't want dinner. I want to take forty sleeping pills and get it over with. But Julie and Andy have been so thoughtful and so loving. We make a big fuss over the dinner. Jerry is feeling just fine—he's gotten a second wind. When I remind them how late it is for us, he urges them to stay longer.

Unable to control myself, at one point I go into the bedroom, take The Letter out of Jerry's coat pocket, take it into the bathroom, read it all. There had been misunderstandings, loss of communication; his letters have been so wonderful—now everything will be straightened out between them. The intimacy so palpable it almost knocks me off the toilet seat. Finally the tears. Oh, my God, the relief to be able to cry after ten hours of knowing. And then no relief at all, for when I can't cry any more, the facts are still there, in my hand. The man I have loved and trusted more than any other human being in the world—the first human being to whom I have expressed *all* my thoughts and feelings—had been lying to me for God knows how long—and *loving somebody else*. Not loving me, naturally, since nobody can be in love with two people at the same time. Making believe he still loved me. Incredible. I must have been in a total coma—for how long?

I wash my face, go back inside, say finally with forcefulness to Julie and Andy, "We *must* get some sleep." We thank them profusely; they leave reluctantly. It has been a source of wonder and delight to us as husband and wife, father and mother, through all the crises of child raising, that this lovely young woman loves *us*! Sheer gravy. Now suddenly, she has no mother or father; I have no husband, no life.

The door closes behind them. I say, "Sit down." I say, "I know. About Nina. I saw the letter while you were reading it, and I have read the rest just now." I begin to scream and to sob. Finally I am shaking from head to foot, my teeth rattling in my head.

WHEN DID YOU STOP LOVING ME?

HOW LONG HAVE YOU LIVED A LIE EVERY SECOND OF OUR LIVES TOGETHER?

WHY? WHY? WHY?

All my life I have felt ugly and undesirable. This has been the only man I have ever allowed to interfere with my closely guarded self-perceptions. He has stabbed me into wailing, helpless agony.

I begin to realize that if I keep on screaming I can't get any answers. I vaguely notice that Jerry's face is stricken. For a fleeting instant I recognize the impossible fact that he is suffering as much as I am, but I push it away—to hell with *that.*

Yes, he says, it is true. About two years. A shock to him, too—it wasn't planned, took him by surprise. Had felt it was almost a father-daughter relationship until . . . He'd gone to her apartment to return some books. She came to the door, weeping of her love. They had been seeing each other often since. Quite often. Once or twice a week, sometimes less. Yes, it was the nights he'd said he was teaching. And then, I'd been traveling a lot, been very preoccupied with my own career. And Julie wasn't living at home any more, and we had each gone our own way, hadn't we?

"So now we get a divorce?" I can't believe the words are coming out of my mouth. We have been through the hinges of hell so many times in our years of marriage, have talked of divorce before, but then it was the two of us fighting for ourselves and each other. Now there is The Intruder, and now the word "divorce" is not a weapon between us, privately, but a kind of social reality. Divorce from me may mean marriage to HER.

Jerry says no, he doesn't want a divorce. He loves me. He cannot explain how this is possible. I shriek that he's crazy, some kind of a pervert. I *know* you can't be in love with two people at one time. I was taught that as a little girl. My mother and father never loved anybody but each other. They were good people; they would never have lied to me about something as important as this. Jerry says, "I know you don't believe it, but it is true."

"Well," I scream. "*I* want a divorce! *This morning!* I never want to see you again. Go pack a bag and get the hell out of here. You are a murderer. I gave my whole life into your hands; I loved you through all your unlovableness—and this is the thanks I get. . . ."

Then, suddenly—the ultimate question. Of course. That's what it's all about. *His* sex problems. The recurrent impotence.

"YOU SONOFABITCH BASTARD, I BET YOU SCREWED HER INTO THE GROUND EVERY TIME —RIGHT? SURE YOU LOVE ME—BUT I GOT ALL THE NEUROTIC SHIT. WHAT DID SHE GET?"

Just as suddenly, the typhoon I am is over. I kneel at the edge of the couch, put my head down, crawl on the couch, whimpering, curl up in a corner, sobbing. I know the answer without his saying a word: no sex problems with Nina.

Suddenly the images start. Oh my God. Jerry making love to her, coming into her, riding her—Hi Ho Silver! What positions did they like best? Would she do things I didn't like? And then the worst of all: afterward, did her head fit into the hollow of his shoulder—in My Place?

I begin to sob uncontrollably. Now the screaming is on the outside. Shrieking—I can't control myself. I hear the howling but hardly know where it is coming from. I see Jerry coming to me on the couch. He looks scared, panic-stricken. He begins to yell at me to stop, but I know he does it to try to get me back from whatever insane place I know I am going. He shakes me, then holds me tight, and the sobbing becomes quieter. He says, "Just one minute. I'm going to go and get you a drink and a tranquilizer."

I have come to the end of feeling. The exhaustion is now greater than the grief. When Jerry comes back, I take the pill, gulp the drink, ask for some sleeping pills. I must have surcease. I try to stand up—I want to get into my bed. My legs are like marshmallow. Jerry practically carries me into the bedroom. He lies down and holds me, rocks me, says over and over again, "I know you don't believe me, but I do love you." The first day is over.

⤳ *SECOND DAY*

"It's the *lying* and *lying* and *lying* I can't believe! I've trusted him so completely. I thought we were closer than any other two people I know!"

I am sitting in Eve's office. I haven't seen her for two years. I'd thought I was finished with psychotherapy—that I'd gone as far as I could go. This morning I woke up feeling half-drugged and yet in piercing pain; it hadn't been a nightmare. I'd taken three sleeping pills, I remembered, and yet I'd only slept four hours. Jerry, looking haggard, was sitting at the kitchen table drinking coffee. I feel as if all the things I want to say are so terrible, so irrevocable, that I'd better not talk at all. We just stare at each other for a moment, and when I begin to cry again, he stands up and puts his arms around me. "I have to see Eve," I tell him.

He asks if he should make the call for me. At first I feel relieved, and then I want to hear her voice. When she answers, I can't talk. I can't stop weeping. "I need to see you right away," I say, finally. She recognizes the desperation. "Jo, whatever it is, we will work on it together," she says urgently, lovingly. "Come at noon."

I feel so weak and numb, I can hardly dress myself. Jerry helps me, as if I am a cripple. He takes me downstairs, holds me in the taxi, says he'll wait for me in the lobby of Eve's apartment building. It is crazy, but I have to admit that some part of me feels loved and cherished. Jerry's suffering and tenderness are so strong that as I ride up in the elevator, I can no longer deny this ambiguity.

Now that I have blurted it all out and used up half the box of tissues on Eve's desk, I suddenly wonder if she's known all along. And then I remember a dream I had had a long time ago.

DREAM

I am living in a house where the living room and kitchen are on an upper level and the bedroom is downstairs. The house is built on a hill. I am lying in bed when I hear a doorbell ring; someone is walking around upstairs. Am afraid to tell Jerry—he might go to investigate, and if there is a robber, he might get killed. The next morning I check my wallet. Some money is gone. Then I remember that the noise did not come from upstairs but from Jerry's side of the bed. I remember there was a woman sort of puttering around there; she is very determined, she wants something and she is determined to get it with as little fuss and noise as possible. The next night I lock up the house very carefully and start down the stairs. Now there seems to be a guest room upstairs, and I see Jerry reading in bed. I ask if he's coming downstairs, and he says no, very clearly and sharply. I realize the same woman is in the bathroom next to the guest room. I begin to feel sexually aroused and wake up.

When I'd had the dream, I remember that I started analyzing it as if the two floors were different levels of my own consciousness, the three characters all different aspects of myself. Suddenly I'd had a thought: Maybe the dream is really a message. Maybe Jerry is having an affair. Eve had looked thoughtful. Gently she had said, "Why don't you ask him?" She had said it as though she were feeling her way, uncertain of my reaction. I had pulled away abruptly. Now I challenge her: did she know?

"I only knew what you told me," she says. "You speak about how terrible it is to know that Jerry lied to you, and I agree that when there is an affair, the real danger to the marriage is the loss of trust. But before you ever had that dream, something else happened. Do you remember telling me about the time you and Julie were shopping together?"

My God. I *had* known. And conveniently repressed the knowledge—for *years!* I can't believe it, but I know it's true.

Julie and I were walking down Fifth Avenue on a shopping spree. It was a snappy, shining fall day. Julie needed some winter clothes, I think. We were on Fifty-sixth Street just about to go past Bonwit Teller's on our way east to Bloomingdale's. Suddenly I'd seen a familiar figure ahead—a tall, lanky man with baggy pants, sloppy jacket, a wild mane of hair. Walking next to him a short girl—younger—taking quick short steps to keep up with him. In an instant I had the feeling he might take her hand. I yelled to catch his attention—he must know we are there before something terrible, irrevocable, happens. He turned, looked shocked, guilty, and uneasy. Covered quickly. Introduces Nina Goodman to us; we talk uncomfortably about having never met. She seems shy, scared, kind of mousy in appearance and manner. If I had been ready then to face my life, I would have known. But I wasn't ready. Now I see that. I remember, with shame, that when we were going to bed that night, I had said, with studied casualness, "You know, today was the first time I ever had the feeling you might be having an affair." Jerry had said nothing. It just hung there—something in the air that I feel now but totally repressed at the time. I hear myself clearly. I said, "If that ever happens, I don't want to know about it."

I hate Eve for reminding me of this episode. She says, "What I knew then and know now is that, while you and Jerry had worked hard to solve your problems, there were lots of things you weren't ready to face. I'm sorry it happened this way, but I'm glad you've come back. We have lots of work ahead of us."

It isn't so much what Eve is saying—it is the way she is looking at me. Warm, compassionate, sure. In spite of the feeling of this being the *end* of my life, there is something in her manner, the love in her eyes, that gets the message through; this is really a new *beginning* of my life.

She sits quietly, letting me weep, letting my anguish, my hurting, pour out. She only stops me when I cry, "He doesn't love me any more!" She says, "Jo, did you ask him?" I acknowledge that I did and that he said he loved me. "But that's not possible," I add. "Nobody can be in love with two people at the same time." Eve is saying something. At first I hear the words but don't understand. She repeats them. "It *is* possible, darling," she says. "*I* have loved two people at the same time."

What is she telling me? She never told me that before. Was she waiting for me to be ready to grow up? What I am mostly aware of in the first minutes after this disclosure is that Eve has given me a gift; knowing my pain, she has opened herself to me, allowed me to see more deeply into her humanness than she ever has before. I wait.

Eve tells me about it. She had married at nineteen—knowing almost nothing about herself. Her husband is ten years older than she. When they'd been married for about five years, she'd met a man in graduate school. She had fallen passionately in love with him, without for a moment wanting to give up her marriage. The affair went on for several years; when she finally felt guilty and conflicted enough to tell her husband, her marriage almost fell apart—not because she had had an affair, but because she had lied. "Trusting was the crucial question; I agree with you that a strong marriage cannot tolerate for very long the breaking of trust. Actually, I think Greg had always felt I married him too young, too little experienced, and that it might well be natural for me to need other relationships from time to time. He's European, and far more open and flexible about such things. We agreed then that we would never lie again. In the thirty-five years of our marriage, each of us has had several love affairs for relatively short periods of time. The other has known about it. Sometimes it has been very painful, but our marriage is stronger than ever. And I think you know I could not be drawn into casual relationships. When it happened it was real loving."

I feel as if some part of the nightmare has lifted; there is a gleam of hope. I love and respect this woman, and she has told me that something I have always thought was impossible, is possible.

When it is time to leave, I tell Eve that I'd like to see her every day for a while. I remember that Jerry is supposed to go to Washington for a few days. We hadn't decided whether or not I would go with him, waiting to see if I'd be too tired after our trip. I am terrified to be left alone, but I have the feeling I need to see Eve a lot right now. Eve says, "Whether or not you go to Washington, I would like you to remember that Jerry has not left you; he's never asked for a separation or divorce; he says he loves you. You can be sure that he has suffered too, and I believe that he is *terrified* at the thought of your leaving him. I know you can't believe that now, but I want you to think about it anyway. Don't push him away, just to get back at him. Maybe you need each other more than you ever did before."

Galien Township Library

2 / 3 00

I am deeply moved by what she has said. The weeping comes again, but it is different. I realize that for the first time I am crying for myself *and* Jerry. When I see him sitting in the lobby, waiting for me, I run to him and we hold each other.

✐ THIRD DAY

We talk about the trip to Washington. I feel I just cannot make the effort. "How can I pretend we are a happily married couple?" I ask. I see something in Jerry's eyes, but I cannot face it. He looks desperate for me to go with him. At the moment, I am wallowing in my own pain and can't yet look at his.

Somehow we go through the motions of living. I call my mother and father, tell them about our trip. They ask, as usual, when they will see us. I tell them Jerry has another trip and I haven't decided about going with him. When I first hear their voices, I want to sob out my suffering, but somehow I manage not to. I know that they would sympathize with me and be furious at Jerry, but in the back of my mind it occurs to me that in some way they will feel it was my fault. I have never felt I measured up to their expectations—I am still too imperfect.

I go out with my shopping cart. I wear dark glasses because the tears keep coming, without control. As I walk up and down the aisles of the supermarket, I wonder if people can tell my husband has been unfaithful. It's like giving up virginity—you wonder if it shows! On my way home, I suddenly feel as if I am wearing a yellow armband as the Jews had to in Germany. I am branded for life—a rejected, abused wife. I realize that I have really believed that Jerry and I would never commit adultery; that was only for people who did not really love each other.

Jerry packs to leave for Washington in the morning. He is very worried about me, asks if he should stay home. He is going on important business—I don't want him to give that up. He starts to say he's not sure he can do it—but stops midsentence. We get ready for bed, exhausted, worn out.

I discover what the hardest time and place is, when we get into bed. For two nights I've been in shock—drugged with pills. Tonight I feel embarrassed, repelled at getting into bed, lying down next to Jerry. I begin to sob again. He wants to hold me, but I scream at him not to touch me. And then, lying alone, isolated, I'm angry at myself. The needing and the hating are unbearable.

And then the images begin—images that will haunt my days and nights for months to come—vivid, agonizing. I see Jerry in bed with Nina, I observe their lovemaking. I wonder if it is totally different with her; do they have private words, special jokes? Suddenly I remember the second night of our marriage. We are in a rooming house near the army camp where Jerry is stationed. As repressed and virginal as I was before marriage, this permission—this marriage license—to suddenly become a sexual being has fallen on rich potential, I discover; Jerry says he knew for sure. In the midst of passion, I suddenly realize that I have slipped backward and my head has gone under a brass rail at the head of the bed; I am now entrapped, imprisoned behind a row of brass rails! We both get hysterical with laughter. It has never occurred to either of us that sex could be funny. It was a wonderful discovery.

Does Jerry tell Nina private things between him and me?

Does he touch her in the same or different ways? How do they kiss? How often have they made love? What has she got that allows a passion without sexual problems for Jerry? I see Nina lying with her head on his shoulder, afterward. That is the worst of all.

I begin to think back. Jerry.has been coming home between ten and eleven at night, two to three times a week. Usually he has gone to bed quickly, but would often wake up in an hour or two, and I would hear him wandering around the house until two or three o'clock in the morning. Sometimes I would get up and yell at him. Sometimes I would ask what was wrong, but as I try to remember, I realize that for quite a while we have had very little contact with each other. When Julie moved out, we almost never had dinner together any more. Jerry was tremendously absorbed in his work—as I was with mine. With Julie gone, I'd felt freer to travel. It had been glamorous, fun. And Jerry wasn't there much anyway. I had traveled quite a lot—even earned more money than Jerry had.

Suddenly I remember—Jerry used to prefer morning showers, but I had noticed and been surprised that he often took showers late at night, for quite a while. Jesus Christ! Was it to wash HER off? How many times did I go to the basement to wash his underwear, when he'd been with HER? Did he ever make love to me on the same *night*? I feel sick with shame and fury. A man living in two houses —two vaginas—I feel a kind of forced intimacy, a physical connection to this Other Woman. She is an infection, a contagion; she has dirtied me.

I try to remember, What's been happening to us lately? What's the sex been like? Come to think of it, there has been less impotence in the last year or so. Some better sex than ever before. (The thought makes me sick.) But on our trip things had degenerated between us. We seemed to be very short-tempered with each other, tired, cranky, unable to really communicate. This had surprised me—usually we loved traveling together and had a marvelous time. When Julie was young, traveling had been the best of romantic times for us. We had even invented other names for ourselves and had played a game that we were lovers, running away from our marriages. What irony that now seems!

As I lie in bed, I realize that I have reached a level of exhaustion that is beginning to frighten me. My inner clock is all out of whack; ordinarily that's enough of a problem, without the shattering of a life in addition. I get up and take two sleeping pills. I want desperately to move over, cling to Jerry, but I can't. It's as if the body of Nina lies between us.

◡◠ FOURTH DAY

Jerry left this morning. He wanted to hold me, kiss me goodbye. I pushed him away. Then, after he'd gone, I was miserable. Suppose the plane crashes and I never see him again? He looked so lost and lonely when he left—his eyes big and sad. Quietly he said good-bye, and, "I really do love you, you know, and I'll come back if you call me. Otherwise we'll talk when I get home."

He's sad? That bastard! Takes this precious marriage of ours and dumps it in the garbage. Nobody in the whole world has tried harder to understand him, be patient with him; no one has ever loved him as I have. Nobody has given him more respect, admiration, encouragement than I. And *he* is upset? To hell with him; to hell with Eve's warnings. I sit down and write him a letter to the hotel in Washington.

> Dear Jerry:
> You are right—we have to talk. We have loved each other so long that in spite of feeling utterly abandoned and shat upon I can see now it would be crazy to run quickly into separation and divorce. I can't think straight, but I do know one thing; the idea of your making love to another woman is so repugnant to me that as long as this affair lasts, I don't want you to touch me. We will talk, and I'll see Eve, and I hope you'll go back into therapy with Margaret, and I am willing to accept the possibility that maybe we can survive this holocaust. I don't really believe that, now, but at the same time I can't believe that all we've put into this marriage can be set aside without at least our making some effort to examine what has happened.
> I hope your meeting goes well. I suppose nothing hurts more than the loss of our companionship, our sharing such events. I thought we appreciated each other so much. I feel defiled, crushed, wounded beyond repair. But I won't rush any decision.
>
> *Jo*

I mail the letter quickly, on my way to seeing Eve. By the time I get to her office, I feel guilty about sending it. Eve suggests that since I have such strong feelings spilling out all over the place, it might make sense to keep a diary, pour out my feelings to myself—and then have the option later of showing it or not showing it to Jerry. She says, "Feeling guilty about what you say or do right now won't serve any useful purpose. You are *in process,* and it is good for you to be in touch with all the feelings you are having. One of these which you are too hurt to acknowledge right now is your feeling for Jerry. All you have ever said about him has made me sense that you care about him very much, and that under your feelings of anger and betrayal there is a part of you that wants to know what has been happening to *him*."

I leave her office in a fury. I hate her! How dare she talk to me about what Jerry feels; she is *my* therapist—I want her to think exclusively about how *I* have been wronged. Maybe I need to see somebody new—somebody not related to the earlier years of our struggle. She seems to be suggesting that this is only the most recent symptom of a troubled marriage, and I think she's crazy.

I get home and lie down on my bed, sobbing. I'm alone, deserted, abandoned. I wish I were dead. My life is over anyway. No matter how long I live, nothing will ever heal this terrible wound I have suffered.

⌒ FIFTH DAY

I can't stop crying. Is it as bad as or worse than if he had died? I think it's worse; I am not only lost and alone, but rejected; feeling not just unbearable grief, but terrible rage.

That tall, handsome, sweet, gentle man that I trusted with my life, that I was able to be more free with, more myself, more open, than with anyone else in the world—the person I trusted as no one else—that monster, that sonofabitch-bastard monster, who professed to care, to understand, to want me to be myself, who took my trust—and then managed to go to another woman, month after month—*years*—God knows how many, really, and in that length and breadth of cheating and deceiving and sharing intimacy with someone else, said clearly and loudly to her and to everyone she told, "My wife does not matter to me enough to be careful, to respect her trust, to be fearful of hurting her terribly. She's so awful, that I need understanding and a different kind of loving. And obviously we don't have a good sex life, or I wouldn't be seeking elsewhere for so long and so well."

This is a superdevil masquerading under The Good and Wise Man, the Devoted Husband. The Good Son. Pretending to care for everyone—and capable of ultimate cruelty to the one person who trusted and loved him more than anyone else in the world.

I want to kill him, torture him, cut off his balls with a slow dull knife. In return for my constant images of his lovemaking with someone else, I'd like to force him to an equal number of daily images of himself, failing in sex with hundreds of girls and women, in front of a large, jeering, laughing audience.

While I sat home, night after night, month after month, feeling cut off, teaching myself to live without sexual feelings, washing his dirty underwear, running his social life, arranging his pleasures, running a big and unnecessary home that I no longer wanted, well and efficiently, spending two or three days of every month paying his bills, taking care of the rent, the insurance, the social correspondence; while I tried to entertain the people that could be important to him, while I tried to keep out of his way, while I sympathized with his fatigue and his heavy workload, that motherfucker was off screwing with some goddamn sonofabitch babe who didn't have to do anything for him but spread her goddamn legs and smile and let him in. She didn't have to get him clean towels or take his phone messages or help him to earn a living, or find clean shirts in the closet or wash his dishes or be pleasant to his relatives or cook his meals. Just cute and quiet and helpless and undemanding—with such a halo around her goddamn head that this stupid miserable ass really thinks she's never had an evil thought for me, or wouldn't like to see me dead. Of course she's so careful and quiet and undemanding—*she* never wanted me to find out —that's why she took the chance of writing to him at a hotel where I might well be picking up the mail! God only knows how many people this little angel has confided in— this waif who makes him feel so strong, this piece of shit who knew damned well, as any woman does, that she, too, was cooperating in the possible destruction of another woman's marriage—someone who had never done a goddamn thing to her.

How do you ever trust again? Why should I try? Why don't I kick the sonofabitch out and tell him I never want to see him again? Let her take over the earning a living, the payments of bills, the running a home, the relatives, the absorption with his feelings, his problems, his needs. Why can't I do it? How can you go on loving and needing someone you hate so violently—someone you now know can hurt you more terribly than anyone you have ever met in your whole life?

It seems vile and dirty and makes me a piece of shit, to be so defiled and not to tell him to get out. What value do I have as a human being? Do I set a value on myself as low as his value of me? Did he always know he could do this with impunity because I loved him too much?

How DARE he lie to me, month after month, year after year, how DARE he let someone else know how little I mattered—and never let me know? I am outraged—I am a good person, I have never knowingly hurt him, I have never done anything that could hurt his public or private image—whatever I have been has been open, whatever I did he knew about, and if he wanted to fight me, he had every invitation to do so—to meet me squarely with the same honesty I offered him. He's a piece of shit—a nothing, a cheat—and the tyranny of the weak and sick is a kind of tyranny I can't possibly match.

Oh my God, how I want him to *suffer*! I just can't think of anything to do to hurt him enough to match the anguish, the horror, that my life has become. He is an evil man, and what I want most is to exorcise him from my life so I can feel some dignity and self-respect again. But I don't believe I can really make him suffer—or more important—*understand* what he has done to me. If I leave him, *I* will suffer the loneliness of the damned—I'll long for him, I will not be able to forget him for a moment, my life will become gray and meaningless—and not because I am a nonperson without him—that just isn't true any more—but because of this goddamn fucking LOVE, which I simply cannot bear another minute. I wish him eternal damnation—and in the same breath, I want him, and need him, desire him with passion, cannot imagine an end to this partnership—even knowing how unreal it has been.

⌁ SIXTH DAY

MY WISHING

Dear God, help me—help me to love what I am, and not to let this perfidy make me see myself as unlovable—ungood, unworthy of respect and protection and caring love. I AM worthy—I am, I am! I have never *knowingly* hurt him or anyone—God give me strength to know all this about him, to somehow accept it as part of what he is, and not let it destroy me.

Let me handle this rage, this hurt, this unbelievable wound—let me grow in understanding, in gentleness, in compassion—somehow to surmount the anger and the pain, somehow to move across it and beyond it, not trying to be strong or powerful or managing to put it all away, nice and neat, but endure and accept and allow it to be in my life, without the obsessional quality it now has, without the pain and the anger.

Please, God, let the hatred for both Jerry and Nina diminish, let me try to understand the human frailty without bitterness, not for their sakes, but for my own, for my survival, for my life ahead, for my becoming something more than I have been—let me accept what is now inevitable and find a place in my insides for it to live without poisoning the rest of my life—let me find some inner peace, and a deeper sense of myself. And, in the end, let me try to help him, let me understand and accept and not blame. And never let me ask for an apology, for some meaningless retribution, some crawling and begging for forgiveness, which will destroy both of us forever.

I can't change him. That is not my task. Let me only change what I can in myself, so that the possibility of such a disillusion is real for me always, that I never again hide myself from this possibility of pain and disaster and loss. Let me know it is always a chance, always a thing that can happen—and that one can live with it, and be glad about being alive.

Let the rage come, let the pain come, let me writhe and die and feel the ultimate torment, let none of it fester and wound me with self-hatred and hating him—let me FEEEL it all, with every pore of my body, let me bathe in the agony, let me experience the depth of my despair, don't let me cut myself off from it, because if I do, it will always be there, killing me half-alive, sick in my gut and my soul.

And let it begin to ebb, let me feel some warm and soothing release, let me be left with my love and my passion, let me want to BE, for myself, for Jerry, for life—let me find the healing thing that can make the pain go away, finally, let it turn into wisdom and understanding, let it leave me with an openness, a yielding, a softness—Oh God, let me be soft out of this—soft, soft, always soft and womanly and never again unknowingly asking for ownership of another human being.

⌒ SEVENTH DAY

Jerry is back from Washington. It was a shock to see him. He looks ten years older—haggard, sad; says it was no fun without me there. In spite of myself, my heart turns over—I can't bear to see him so unhappy. I want to kill him, but I don't want to look at his suffering!

We are wary with each other; we are walking on eggs. There is an uneasy self-consciousness. Being separated for a few days seems to have left us sort of hanging midair, not knowing what to do next. I tell Jerry I'm sorry about the letter I wrote. He seems relieved, says he tore it up. That makes me mad at first; then I'm glad. It is obvious neither of us has the vaguest idea of what we will feel from moment to moment.

Jerry says he has to go to the office to check his mail. My

immediate reaction is that he is going to call Nina—probably arrange to see her. I feel as if I will die if he goes to her this evening, and so I say, "Jerry, we've *got* to talk. Please come home early tonight." He agrees quickly, willingly. I want so badly to touch him, hug him; it's an ache. I go out to the hall with him to wait for the elevator. He searches my face, and then says, "You're not wearing a flowered negligee." It's an old joke; we once knew a woman who said she always went to the door to see her husband off in the morning, wearing a pretty flowered negligee. "After all," she had said, in a honeyed southern drawl, "One just nevah knows if one will evah see one's beloved again." We had met few couples who hated each other more. The memory of how often we had laughed about this—and imitated her—shakes us; we are both in tears. We rush to each other and cling as we hadn't allowed ourselves to when Jerry had come home. We are both weeping and go back into the apartment to recover before Jerry leaves. I want to touch him more than ever. Suddenly we are both caught up in a kind of wild passion that hasn't happened for a long time. There is a savagery in our lovemaking. We are two separate people, each experiencing our own needs without any tender regard for the other. It has a kind of inexorability about it—a wildness. We both cry and laugh and there is no need for words.

Afterward Jerry says, "I guess the office can wait until tomorrow. If you want to, let's talk now. Or after you make me a Big Feast—like a dozen eggs, a pound of bacon, and eight cups of coffee!" Suddenly we realize it is the first time in a week either of us have thought about food or been hungry · We both go to the kitchen, and after we have eaten like a couple of starving wolves, we sit at the kitchen table. We both know that this will probably be the most important conversation we have ever had.

DIALOGUE (*A Digest!*)

ME: The dumb part of my brain is obsessed with the physical relationship. But I know that is not the most important part. What will always hurt the most was the *lying*. We worked so hard, at so many problems—so openly and honestly. . . .

JERRY: That's not completely true.

ME: What do you mean?

JERRY: I believe that you always told me how *you* were feeling, but I was keeping a lot of *my* feelings to myself. I was scared of you. I have always loved you, but there have been many times when I was angry. . . .

ME: Then why in hell didn't you *tell* me?

JERRY: For a lot of reasons. First of all, it is much harder for me to even know what I'm feeling. Sometimes I can't figure out a feeling for days or weeks—or even months after I've had it. Part of it we did talk about; the fact that you had a much happier childhood than I did, that expressing feelings was easier for you. But I never could tell you how much I was suffering.

ME: What did you think I would do?

JERRY: First of all, you suffered enough for both of us. Don't you think I knew—all the tears—when I was impotent? I wanted to kill myself. I can recall vividly every goddamn time it happened; every bed, every hotel, every town. I can remember the *wallpaper* in the rooms! I felt like a total failure *all the time*. After a few days, you would bounce back and be fine; I never got over any of it.

ME: My God! Lots of the time I thought you just weren't interested in sex, and mostly I felt I was unattractive, undesirable—so it couldn't be your fault.

JERRY: After all the really bad periods, you would get

hysterical, and I would reassure you that I loved you—
and in a day or two you'd be fine. I would go right on
feeling ashamed, tormented, furious at myself. . . .

ME: You mean all these years? Until—Nina?

JERRY: Nina was sort of an accident. It was nothing I
planned or thought about in advance, but when it happened, I realized that all the time I had had the feeling
that if I couldn't solve that problem, I would kill myself.

ME: So my feelings about myself were true; you just
needed someone who attracted you, more. . . .

JERRY: No, that's not true. I have always found you the
most desirable woman I ever met. I think it was because
you mattered so much—but there have always been so
many *conditions* in loving you.

ME: What's that supposed to mean?

JERRY: From the very beginning. I wish I could have told
you, but I couldn't. You never understood about our
meeting each other. When we met, I could not recall
ever having had a feeling of love before. My childhood
was just a big blank. Remember—I could barely answer
the simplest questions about my family? Well, the moment I saw you, something happened to me. For the first
time that I could remember I was flooded with warmth—
it must have been love, but I didn't know what love
was. All I knew was that I wanted to be with you, to
make love to you, and that if you would say yes, it
would change my whole life. . . .

ME: Never once, in the first two years after our meeting,
did you ever use the word "love." If you had, it might
have been different. You just told me you liked me a lot
—and that wasn't enough for me.

JERRY: I know. It's a little late to tell you, but now I
think it was some kind of a test. I couldn't say I loved

you—I had no idea what such words meant. I only knew that you were the person I wanted to be with, and that if you responded I might come alive.

ME: Jesus! And I was such a prig! All that talk about waiting to get married. But naive and repressed as I was, I think I might have been different if only you'd said it was love.

JERRY: You thought I was just a fresh kid seeing how much I could "get." It wasn't that at all. It just seemed so *right*. As if your going to bed with me would tell me something I had been waiting to find out all my life. . . .

ME: You mean unconditional love. . . .

JERRY: Yes, exactly.

ME: My God, if I had only understood . . .

JERRY: I was terrified of getting married. All I knew about it was that it was horrible, that people destroyed each other. But it seemed to be the only way—a bargain. You would love me if I married you. I wanted you to love me even if I didn't marry you.

ME: [*beginning to weep*] I loved you so much I couldn't think about anything else after our second or third date. When you were away in the army, my entire day centered on whether or not I got a letter from you. I couldn't believe anyone could love me enough to marry me. By then I was twenty-one and my mother was getting nervous! I was terrified of being an old maid.

JERRY: What I learned in therapy was that by the time we actually got married, I was in a rage. It was the bargain part of it. Under the surface of my life I had almost always felt a profound depression, and it deepened after the wedding. On the one hand I was angry that I'd had to "buy" your loving me with a wedding license, and I was depressed because it confirmed what I already felt about myself; no one could ever love me without conditions. I lived with that feeling until Nina, who made no conditions.

ME: This is the most incredible conversation. I can't believe it. We talked so many times about how unhappy you were as a child. I was the one who urged you to see a therapist. And all the years you were seeing Margaret and unearthing these feelings—why didn't you tell me then, for God's sake?

JERRY: You are really a very formidable lady! I don't think you have ever realized it, but lots of times Julie and I have both been scared of you. You express your feelings so easily—and so noisily! Nobody could ever wonder what's on your mind—it's all right there, on the surface. Julie and I are both more introverted. You made us feel powerless, helpless. You were always more competent; everybody liked you; you were so successful in your work. I loved you, but I was scared of you.

ME: I can't *believe* it; you, above all people, knew the truth about my feelings of inadequacy and unworthiness—all the self-hatred . . .

JERRY: Yes. But somehow, because you could talk about it and I couldn't, I always felt you were the strong one. I was always afraid of you.

ME: This is known as the tyranny of the weak. I was strong, you were scared—so you destroyed my life. . . .

JERRY: You see what's happening? I'm trying to be more honest with you than I have ever been before, and you are getting furious and sarcastic. . . .

ME: No, I'm not; I only *sound* that way. Inside I am shaking with pain. I love you so much and I seem to have done nothing but hurt you. I thought loving you had helped you; now it seems it only did you harm. . . .

JERRY: That's not true. If I had never met you I would have been a robot, an automaton. That's what I was. I had a good brain for thinking, but no feelings. I would have become a mathematician or a computer programmer, I suppose. I can't imagine ever having gotten married. Your strength pulled me into life. As I've told you, I never saw anything in color until I met you. The world was all in black and white. It was such a shock when I began to see colors! You gave me life. And you *did* give me love—the only love I ever had. Aside from these things I could never say to you, it is also true that I owe my life to you.

ME: Which I guess is another reason to feel anger toward me. . . .

JERRY: Yes, in the sense that, as time went on, I began to feel that everything I was, I owed to you, that there was no part of me that really belonged to myself. That's why I began to insist on going away by myself sometimes. I was trying to find out if I existed without you.

ME: Jerry—the one thing I hear loud and clear is that you have a new strength I never used to hear; it's as if you have a new hunger for more feeling—strong enough, finally, to say what you have needed to say. . . .

JERRY: [*tears in his eyes—he stands up and looks down at me*] Yes! Yes! I was crippled for so long; I saw myself as a horrible monster. And I couldn't go on living unless I could change that. . . .

ME: And part of it was freeing yourself from my domination. . . .

JERRY: I guess I'd have to say yes to that. But remember— the feeling of domination wasn't what kept me with you. If I hadn't loved you and needed you, I could have just gotten up and left. I never wanted to do that—except for short vacations!

ME: You know what I'm thinking about? [*I can hardly get it out—the sobbing—*] Remember the time I went to see you in the army? The hotel, and my insistence that we get separate rooms? By that time I was so in love with you, I could have overcome my fears and my inhibitions if only you had said you loved me. . . .

JERRY: Darling—I didn't know what love *was!* All I knew was that I wanted you. . . .

ME: And I talked about marriage!

JERRY: Well, that was a long time ago. Since then we have both accepted and understood you couldn't have done anything else, given your parents and the attitudes you were taught.

ME: It was a long time ago—but it seems to have affected our lives a lot. The impotence was partly unexpressed anger at my conditional love, partly depression at having your worst fears about yourself realized, partly a feeling of being owned by a dominating woman. . . .

JERRY: Listen—you don't have to get so clinical about it. What I was trying to explain was that when I saw you, from the very first moment, I was so sure this was *right*—that if you wanted it as much as I did everything would change for me, forever. Now we know there were things which blocked both of us. But our troubles only began that way. The truth is that I *never* could understand why someone like you could love me, and not being able to tell you what I felt was because I was sure that if you ever knew the real me, you'd leave me. . . .

ME: My God! I never, ever loved anyone the way I love

you. No matter how bad it ever was, being with you was always better than being without you. How could you not know that? I never walked away—I stayed in the struggle; and we had some wonderful times. . . .

JERRY: Rationally—sure. No matter how I failed, you never left me. But I always thought you might. . . .

ME: And all the time I was thinking that maybe you wanted to get rid of me, but I couldn't let go; that I was unlovable. . . .

JERRY: We have hurt each other for only one reason: because we thought so little of ourselves.

ME: And we have tried so hard to change that. . . .

JERRY: Look—we haven't failed. I think we've made a lot of progress. . . .

ME: *This* is progress? My God, what are you going to do to me next?

JERRY: You see—it's what *I* am going to do to *you*. That's why I can't tell you how I feel.

ME: Believe me, you've done very well, at last.

JERRY: I guess we'd better stop. . . .

It has all been too much for me. I feel shocked, confused, hurt—and yet in some strange way, relieved. I have seen Jerry in a different light. He is stronger than ever before. I have to adjust to this. I find I respect him in a new way. He has been able to talk back! I tell him I need time to think over what he has said. We are very quiet with each other. When we go to bed, there is no touching, no contact; we could be total strangers.

✑ EIGHTH DAY

This morning the quietness continued. We barely talked; Jerry left early for his office. I sat in the kitchen, crying by myself—unable to stop. Then I began to remember our beginnings—those first meetings—the sense of immediacy, something happening between us—and my forcing it into a pattern of expectations, demands, promises. Suddenly I am overwhelmed with regret. That poor, sad young man—never loved, terrified of life, unaccustomed to feelings—and I pushed him away. If only I could have held out my arms, if only I had been so sure of myself that I could have said "I love you" without having to wait for him to say it first. I *knew* what love was; I recognized it right away. What kind of a dumb-ass scared kid was I, that *I* couldn't have told *him?*

I go to the telephone and call his office. I can hardly talk. But somehow I say, "I'm sorry I wasn't strong enough to give you unconditional love from the moment we met. I want to now. All of a sudden, I know that I want you and need you and love you, and it doesn't matter what you do. You can screw twenty girls in Macy's window, and I'll still want you to come home to me." Jerry bursts into wracking sobs at the other end of the line. We listen to each other crying; neither of us can talk. Finally, almost talking to myself, I wonder aloud, "Can human beings survive having such terrible regrets?" Jerry says, "Nothing else matters but what you just said to me. It is the most important thing you ever said."

He says he'll come home as soon as he can.

✑ *NINTH DAY*

Today it is as if yesterday never happened. I feel angry, miserable, all closed up again. It seems incredible—these tremendous shifts from such passion and closeness to anger and suffering.

Jerry told me this morning that he was starting to see Margaret again. In fact, he has been seeing her, off and on, for several years—more often, I guess, than I was actually aware of. A number of times now Jerry has talked about his depression; does he mean he's been depressed all his life, or something specific, related to these past few years? Probably both.

I've never really met Margaret—to talk to her. She was recommended to Jerry by Eve a few years ago when I was seeing Eve regularly. At that time, she had one session with Jerry and me together and told him she thought he was very depressed. Jerry and I met Margaret at the theater several years ago. She made me feel uncomfortable, uneasy—I don't know why. But Jerry liked her right away. Now I hate her. She has known, all this time, that he was having an affair! I hate her for not telling him to cut it out—and I am so ashamed and embarrassed. She must know all my failures, all my shortcomings. Maybe she thought Nina was better for Jerry than I was.

Jerry feels she has helped him a great deal. When he tells me this, I become sarcastic and furious. "Yes," I say, "it's wonderfully clear that she's done you a world of good. Unfortunately, her helpfulness has brought me to the brink of the total destruction of my life!"

This morning I knew that Jerry woke up wanting to talk some more about what I'd said on the phone yesterday. Yesterday was full of hope for renewal, and he tried to tell me how much it meant to him. I can't rise to the occasion. I tell him I meant what I said, but today I feel miserable again. During the night there were all those images of him with Nina; I am still tortured by her presence.

Jerry looked so sad—disappointed in me, I guess. He hesitated at the door, didn't know what to say, then tells me he will come home for supper if I want him to, but must then go to a meeting. I tell him not to do me any favors. His face closes—we have lost each other again. I can't bear it. I wait a half hour—restless, agitated—and then call him at his office as soon as I think he'll have gotten there. When he answers, I say, "Look, nothing has changed about what I said yesterday. If you want to get a divorce, I'll live in sin with you for as long as you want me to! I wish I'd done it from the day we met, now that I understand you needed that as a message of loving so badly. I'm glad about the things you've said to me. But now I feel you are expecting too much of me. Goddamn it, I'm *bruised*—I'm hurting like I never hurt before. I can't help it. Don't try to rush me."

I spend the whole day in tears again—partly at least because of Jerry's sad and lonely voice when he thanked me for calling.

I think my mother knows what has happened. She called this morning, and I just couldn't stop crying or hide my gloom. I realize her reaction tells a lot about my attitudes. When I didn't want to define my pain she said, "Is it the worst?" That's her definition of adultery! I felt two messages coming through: the first was protective, compassionate, fury at Jerry for hurting me. The second was loud and clear: when and how had I gotten lazy about my marriage? "I've been telling you for years," she said, "that you don't pay enough attention to your appearance." The roots of self-hatred, forever and ever—implanted in my soul. "We mustn't let Daddy know," she says. "It would break his heart."

◡◔ TENTH DAY

This is the first day I am to see my parents since we came home from our trip. Especially after yesterday's conversation with my mother, I wake up full of dread and foreboding. Again I begin to cry and can't stop. I want to be a little girl and have my parents take care of me. I want to be in bed sick and have them bring me ice cream; I want to show them a scratched knee and have them kiss it.

I keep crying and crying. We are going to their house for dinner. Other relatives will be there. I start screaming that I can't go, I can't face them, I'll die. Jerry gets angry, shouts at me to stop carrying on. I scream louder. He slaps my face. Time stops for both of us; he has never done that before. We are both appalled. He turns away, begins to sob, kicks the closet door, pounds the top of his dresser. I crawl back into bed, holding my face. It really hurts. I cry more quietly. I want to stop but I can't. Jerry comes over, tries to turn my face. "Oh God," he says, and goes into the kitchen. I hear him taking out ice trays. He comes in with an ice pack and tells me to put it on my eye. I realize I must be getting a black eye!

Jerry crawls into bed beside me, holding the ice pack very gently, his dry, racking sobs mingling with my weeping.

Over and over again I say, "I can't go, I can't face them," all the time knowing I must, that it can't be avoided. I realize it is time to get dressed. How in the name of God will I explain a black eye? My mother will probably call the police and have Jerry arrested!

After a while we both sit up. I go to look in the mirror. There is a slight swelling, but no discoloration. I could put a Band-Aid on my cheek and just say I have a bad pimple or something.

I look at Jerry. He looks tormented. I begin to move toward him as he sits on the edge of the bed. I hold out my arms, cradle his head against me. He murmurs, "My dearest dear."

It is a thunderbolt. Those were the words of greeting in Nina's letter to him. He has chosen the only three words in the whole English language that he must never say to me. What demon, what monster brought them to his lips at this moment? I shriek in such pain that the neighbors must have thought I was having a leg amputated without an anesthetic, or that someone was holding an acetylene torch next to my body. That's how I feel. I race into the bathroom and lock the door. I am going to take every sleeping pill, every tranquilizer I can find; or if I can't find enough, I will take one of Jerry's razor blades and cut my wrists.

I hear Jerry screaming, then kicking the door. He kicks it in. He's like a wild maniac. We scream and tear at each other, sobbing.

Exactly one hour and forty-three minutes later, we ring the bell of my parents' apartment. We are late, and all the other relatives are there already. We greet everyone gaily; only my mother searches my face anxiously, looks daggers at Jerry until I whisper to her to stop it. Nobody notices anything is wrong.

⌒ *ELEVENTH DAY*

I brought a dream in to my session with Eve this morning.

DREAM

Jerry and I are on a plane. He has an aisle seat, and suddenly, when I turn my head to look at him, I see a young woman curled up in his lap. She is very jolly and cuddly—seems absolutely delighted to be where she is. She explains to me that she does this all the time and has some wonderful experiences.

I am furious and try to push her off. She doesn't get angry—is perfectly affable—but won't budge. She does exactly what she pleases, no matter how nasty I become.

I seem to meet her in other places—not sure where—but I begin to have the feeling she is someone I must reckon with. In spite of myself, I find her sensual, womanly—charming, even. I feel my dislike is unreasonable, but I still behave very badly toward her. At one point she tries to pat me on the arm, and I recoil and scream, "Don't touch me!"

Eve is smiling broadly when I finish telling her the dream. She makes me mad. "What's so funny?" I ask. "This is a reenactment of the agony I've been living through."

"I don't think so," she said. We let it go for a while, but when it is time for me to leave, she says, "Why don't you write a dialogue between yourself and that woman in your dream? I think it would be helpful." I hate the idea and have no intention of doing anything about it. But here I am, two hours later, and I guess I'm going to try it.

DIALOGUE (*A Fantasy*)

ME: I guess I can't put it off; I must confront you. Who are you?

OTHER WOMAN: You know perfectly well who I am. And it's about time you had a talk with me. I've had a few things to say to you, too. If you had put this off much longer, you might have destroyed both of our lives, for good. . . .

ME: What are you talking about? I never saw you before in my life. . . .

OTHER WOMAN: Come on, now, don't be ridiculous! I'm the one you've been calling a whore, a sexual pervert, a nymphomaniac. I'm the one you think could have turned you into a famous Madam—a courtesan, sitting on a chaise longue in an eighteenth-century boudoir being served little cakes by a French maid. . . .

ME: You are crazy. I know perfectly well who you are; you are Nina.

OTHER WOMAN: I'm your cliché. You have invested me with the most romantic qualities and the most despicable ones. You are scared to death of me—and you have been since you were a little girl. You would have killed me if you could have, but you never could quite manage it. Inside that tight-ass, virginal little prude there always lurked just enough abandoned animal. . . .

ME: You talk in such riddles. I'm not going to try to figure out who you are. But I must admit I find myself wondering why you seem to like yourself so much. I can tell from your manner with both me and Jerry that you enjoy being a woman and see yourself as very attractive —desirable. I'd like to know what makes you that way, because I am so much the opposite. I see myself as so ugly, unlovable. . . .

OTHER WOMAN: Jerry loves you. . . .

ME: I know that, and instead of feeling reassured, I wonder what's the matter with him. Any time any man comes in my direction, I immediately assume he's blind or stupid.

OTHER WOMAN: The difference between us is of your own making. What you call disgusting, I call young, passionate, beautiful; what you call irresponsible, I call wild, alive—good. What you call whorish, I call earthy, lusty.

ME: There *is* something familiar about you, but I can't quite recall where we have met. Did we go to college together? There was a girl down the hall from me who was the most abandoned creature I'd ever seen. If she wasn't out screwing, she was in her room masturbating. I remember she used to use a Coke bottle—she was revolting, disgusting. . . .

OTHER WOMAN: You were so jealous, you could hardly stand it. . . .

ME: That's a lie. I hated her. . . .

OTHER WOMAN: No, you were afraid of her. You had this childish idea that sexual feelings would make you behave the same way she behaved. Of course, it wasn't true at all, but that has always been your problem. This idea that allowing the full range of one's sensual being means becoming a whore. I must tell you that it was a great surprise to me that even within the safety and propriety of the marriage bed, you were able to allow yourself some pleasures at long last. . . .

ME: Are you suggesting that you have been *watching* me? You are some kind of dangerous maniac. You have got to be put away. . . .

OTHER WOMAN: Yes, I know; you have managed to do that very well. . . .

ME: Someone like you can destroy civilized relationships.

OTHER WOMAN: Someone like you can destroy life and loving. . . .

ME: You make me afraid. What do you want of me?

OTHER WOMAN: Only that you know who I am and let me in. . . .

ME: I know who you are. I can't let you in.

OTHER WOMAN: You are not only a silly child—that was unfair of me. You are also a talented, creative, lovely person. You know some things about loving, and you might even be a very good writer someday—but honestly, and truly, and with love—you can't do it without letting me in. . . .

ME: I'm so afraid of you. I always have been. I'm shaking with terror right this minute, because if you don't disappear right now I am going to recognize you, and there is still a part of me that cannot bear to do it. . . .

OTHER WOMAN: That's all right. I'll leave now. But I feel more hopeful. We have been closer than we have ever been before.

I sit here, shivering and shaking. I know that when I take this dialogue to Eve tomorrow, I will have to go on discovering this other part of myself. Do I have enough courage? I am so scared. And yet I know I have to do it. I want so desperately to be whole, all alive—nothing denied.

⌒ *TWELFTH DAY*

I keep wondering if Jerry's seen her since we came back from our trip. I feel instinctively he hasn't. but that's probably wishful thinking. I think he's in conflict about it all—he seems tired and upset.

Ever since we got home I've had the feeling that I'm winning the war between my rigid self and newer self; I'm coming close to a new way of feeling about love and marriage. It's still fuzzy, confused, but I feel it happening—almost against my own will.

But there is also so much anger and sadness—even after all the crying and howling. It still hits me like a ten-ton-weight, that there were years of really quite terrible deceiving—of a nature that just utterly horrifies me. And *not* because we hated each other, or weren't constantly trying to reach each other. Even in our most separated periods, we were still closer than most people ever are. All during these years I was sharing everything I felt, everything that was important to me. We were touching and loving as much or as often as he wanted to—and all that time he knew he was doing something that would break my heart and my soul and damn near kill me if I knew about it.

I am afraid to come too quickly to understanding and forgiving. He will have gotten off too easily. Never did a man have a more understanding wife! I figured out all the reasons, blaming myself for all my failings, justified it, tied it all up in a neat package—it was the malaise of our marriage,

I'm as much to blame as he—I will change my expectations and attitudes; no more conditions—I'll just love him.

Now I see that I am still the one who does the fastest and best growing and changing—he falls far short of where I go; he remains secretive, inarticulate, unable to follow up on clues to his own growth. He is retreating back into his work now; what further problem could there be? He has one of the biggest and most erect penises in captivity; it performs admirably—what in the world could I possibly complain about?

I'm getting good and mad. I have the feeling that the act of sex is now supposed to justify the deception, the cheating, the infidelity—all the things it still was. I am the benefactress of this wonderful thing he did for me. Shit on him! Sex without love is not for me—and love means compassion and not wanting to hurt someone you care about. I feel frightened. It is marvelous, having such a wonderful time with sex—I was awash with loving feelings—and now I wonder *why*; what made me feel so loving, when he was the source of so much pain?

⌒ *TWO WEEKS*

I feel as if some initial frenzy is over. There is less feeling of being threatened—I know Jerry doesn't want to leave me; I know he still wants to make love to me. Now I find myself drawing away. It began by my not having an orgasm; I realized I was detached. Now I know that anger is coming back, but not like before. Not a hot rage, but cold fury.

When Jerry begins to touch me, I feel I will be betraying some important thing in my self if I respond. I am back to feeling violated on every level. I try to be honest about how I feel, but Jerry is exhausted and can't hear me. If I talk about it, he gets angry, depressed.

As I look back, it now seems as if the first shock was not as bad as this period. I feel as if I have struggled so hard to accept what happened—and now I want it to be *over!* Now that I understand some of the things that were bothering Jerry, why doesn't he give Nina up? There is no indication from him that this has happened. Isn't he grateful for how hard I've tried to change? Does Nina still fill some needs I don't? I realize that we seem to be in a silent struggle in which I cannot have my own way. Part of me still wants to threaten that I will leave if he doesn't end the affair. Part of me feels hurt and angry that we go on, together—on his terms.

Jerry has just moved to a new office, and I have been furnishing it for him. I found some excellent secondhand pieces, including a nice couch; the only thing that was wrong with it was that it opened up into a bed! While Jerry was out of town, I waited in his office for the air conditioner man to come. I found pajamas and a bathrobe in his office closet. How cozy! I have provided him with a love nest! I know he sometimes sleeps in the office when he wants to work very late—but what else? Do they make love on the couch I bought? How does she touch him? Kiss him? Is she very sophisticated in sex? Do they do things we never tried? Is it serious or sometimes funny? Is it really possible that she asks for nothing, hopes for nothing, or is Jerry deluding himself? Is she suffering?

I simply cannot imagine being in love with two people at the same time. If you love someone, well, that's who you love. It's secret and private and all-embracing; *total.* You want to own each other's lives, make each the center of the other's world. Is that really so awful? How can our intimacies be only ours if a piece of Jerry is hidden in mystery, unknown. I am not a companion, a sharer in his life, when something as real as loving somebody else is between us. If she's going to be there, in our lives, then it seems to me she should share the miseries as well as whatever joys. Let's include *her* in our money problems! Let *her* share in all the other parts of life—laundry, cooking, fatigue, discouragement, crankiness, annoyances with demanding relatives, family crises—all of it. Why should she only share in the good things? I wonder if Jerry and Nina have their own share of bad things. Do they fight, turn against each other? Probably not; they aren't together enough! That's what it's all about, I guess; *not* having to spoil love with daily living!

I feel as if sooner or later I will just stop loving him. He hurts me too much. Can you just go on being hurt and still loving—endlessly? And yet, I must admit I see changes in Jerry! He's kind of a bull of a man, part of the time at least —glowing in his sexuality, making up for a lifetime of anxiety and frustration. And it is true that I never had any idea of the depths of his torment. Now he is exultant—a sexual powerhouse! And I find myself getting perverse; instead of enjoying it, it makes me mad. Is it a package deal? Can he only be like this if Nina is part of it? I wish I had the guts to leave him, to start a new life on my own.

The ending of the impotence isn't just sexual. I think Jerry has a sense of power in general. He is making the rules, doing what he wants to do whether I like it or not; he's running the show. I can't stop him. Is this something he has needed all along? I can't believe that I will endure it forever —I hope I won't.

I am ashamed to admit it, but sometimes I feel that I would rather have gone on living the old way—with the sexual problems, with Jerry's "black moods," with the loss of communication. Nothing was as joyful as the best moments now—but nothing was as painful, either. The pain of the infidelity seems worse than what we had before. He had to change, move on—but I think I probably could have stayed where we were. Jerry is forcing me to change, and I bitterly resent it being his choice, not mine.

Last night (second late night this week), Jerry said he had to see Margaret and wouldn't be home for supper. He came home about nine. I paced the floor and wondered, and hated the thought of being lied to again, but I wasn't sure.

If he did break off with Nina, would he tell me? It seems to me it would be the depth of cruelty not to. It also seems insane that I know nothing about what is happening, nothing about such an important part of his life.

I found a pair of woman's glasses on Jerry's dresser this morning. My immediate thought is that Nina asked him to put them in his pocket and he forgot about it. This is always my first point of reference. When he finally got home, Jerry told me he walked for three hours, then had a hamburger and coffee. I couldn't control myself—I told him I didn't believe him. He became very angry and defensive—so I told him not to protest, I wouldn't believe him. We both shut up and moved away from each other, each of us being aware that we were on the verge of saying things we would regret. Later it seemed to me he was looking at me strangely—sort of a fierce expression on his face. He looks uncertain, as if he is about to say something. Then he takes a shower and washes his own underwear. I immediately assume that he and Nina have been together.

I just cannot go on this way. It is too painful. We are

so much to each other—there is such loving—and then, also, so much that isn't being said; the burden is just too much for me. I *can't* maintain this love-freedom thing.

✑ *THREE WEEKS*

I am in the blackest despair. Jerry won't tell me anything, and he won't give her up. I feel as if *I* am now only worthy of conditional love. For so many years of our marriage I felt like half a woman because of his sexual difficulties; I was not attractive to him. Now I am—but only if he can have someone else on the side. If only I could die without having to do it myself. Right now I think I would feel relieved if someone told me I had a fatal form of cancer.

I can't stop weeping. Jerry closes up, moves away, looks angry and miserable. We can't go on like this. Last night I dreamed of Nina. She seemed calm and happy. Very cheerful and not at all troubled by my rage and misery.

Eve's interpretation of the dream is that my unconscious is ahead of my conscious! She says I'm in better shape than I am willing to acknowledge. That Nina was really myself —recovering, looking ahead. I know she 's right, and it makes me furious!

If Jerry doesn't really love her as much as he loves me, what is so precious and important about it. Yesterday he blurted out "It's almost ended twice." Which one is clinging to it? Does Nina have any other men in her life? Is she crying, afraid she's losing? My God, how I wish she'd find someone new and kick Jerry out!

It *would* help if he could give me some understanding

of what the relationship is. Mystery is harder to endure—I imagine so much more than what the reality probably is. I think more and more (as so much pain wears me down) of the reality of our separating. How shocked people would be! Everyone thinks we have such a model marriage. I feel I can't go on with our lovemaking. Maybe I ought to end that part of our lives. It would be a deprivation—but also a relief; it would express more of my real feelings.

Life seems meaningless without him, and yet I want to make him suffer. I still think about punishing him—and suicide.

How do you dissolve a marriage of more than a quarter of a century? What about all the accumulated memories and possessions? Every book, every painting, has its own history, shared by us. We *are* like one person in so many ways; we've lived through so much together. How do you start to pull it all apart? Especially when you just can't really hate each other.

Jerry has changed so much. His interests, the people around him, his work, his attitudes, the way he approaches people. I sense that change is all that lies ahead of me, and I am so frightened.

I have the feeling I am very close tonight to being able to take enough sleeping pills to finish it all. You reach a point where pain is ALL of you, and death seems a reasonable and inevitable surcease. But something holds me back. I wish it didn't. I walk aimlessly from room to room, endlessly weeping. I feel so utterly alone.

Last night Jerry came home, took a shower, and washed his underwear before eating supper. I can't help it—I start wondering if he was with Nina. Jerry must be longing for the day when I leave town on my business trip. It must be difficult to have two women in the same city, when you have to see both of them on the same days. When I leave, he'll have a perfect setup. How much longer can I stand living like this?

Jerry came back from seeing Margaret, looking awful. Very depressed, eyes bloodshot; suddenly I feel waves of compassion. He's no cruel monster, he's a hurting human being whom I love. He tells me he feels as if he has arthritis of the soul: *old*. He tells me nothing is going well. I feel that my unhappiness is causing him too much guilt and grief. Maybe it's a sign of progress when he can tell me he's in pain.

Jerry is *really* upset today—very depressed, sad, unable to talk to me about what's going on. He woke up stiff, with a pain in his back. I guess it's progress when he somatizes in these normal ways when he's tense! Of course, I'm wondering if his mood might have anything to do with maybe breaking up with Nina. If it is, I have mixed feelings. I don't want him to feel old and despairing; what do I gain from his suffering? I guess I would rather endure the affair than see him looking so desolate—destroyed. And to make it all worse, he brought me a bunch of lilacs—the first he's seen—since he knows how much I love them. He told me that in part he's feeling angry because he can't blame any of his troubles on me any more! "Whenever I felt depressed or miserable before, I could always assure myself it was because you were making impossible demands; I can't lay my trip on you any more—and that infuriates me!"

↝ *FOUR WEEKS*

I am sobbing in Eve's office; why should *I* be treated so shabbily? My father would *never* do what Jerry has done to me. Eve says, "Why don't you write about your father?"

THE MAN I HAVE KNOWN BEST—
OR AT LEAST LONGEST

My father is a very honorable man; my husband is not. My father is incapable of hurting anyone he loves. He could never be unfaithful to his wife. He could not be so cruel. My husband has no such sensitivity—he doesn't care what he does to me. I feel betrayed, unloved, belittled. I remember once, long ago, having a discussion with my father about marital fidelity. Maybe I already suspected, at least unconsciously, what was happening; maybe I was testing the water—to see if I could endure such knowledge. I remember saying to him that I thought a wise and mature woman ought to tolerate infidelity if she wants her husband to reach his fullest potential as a human being; she can't make conditions of servitude. My ordinarily polite and proper father had responded quite violently. "That's a lot of crap!" he said, much to my astonishment. His passion surprised and—I guess—delighted me. "That's a wonderful rationalization for a man to do anything he feels like doing, no matter how it affects other people." He adds, "If you really love a person—man or woman—you could never hurt him or her that much."

That was exactly what I wanted to hear. I wish some-one felt that way about me now. How wonderful to be so cherished, so protected from pain! I feel grateful, comforted, just to think that there is one man at least who could understand this awful wound.

In spite of myself I find myself thinking about my mother—and this great, protective love she has. Would I want it? What has it done for her? She is a child-woman; a spoiled child; my father is her slave. He's afraid of her. I don't think I have ever heard him cross her—she does all the yelling, complaining, demanding; he does the placating. They love each other—but has my father ever fulfilled *his* potential? Christ, no.

There is a price to be paid for having a perfectly de-voted husband who disregards his own needs to satisfy his wife. My mother is so often petulant, angry, un-happy—discontented. Sometimes I've had the feeling it would have done her a world of good to get a good spanking. Her demands are endless; the more my father tries to please her, the more it never seems to be enough. She is like some bottomless pit of needs and wants. (My God, is that what I've been like all these years? Is this what Jerry has been afraid to tell me? Did I get a "spanking" I deserved?)

To hell with that. I feel unloved, betrayed, hurt. I want to be loved exclusively and forever like my mother. I am shocked beyond sanity to have been so attacked; I hate my life, my work. I want to die from shame; I want oblivion.

But do I have any other kinds of feelings? Do I really want what my mother has? Suddenly I feel very proud that never, in all the years of our marriage, have I ever allowed Jerry to set any limits on the possibilities of his own professional fulfillment. I have sometimes asked for safety and comfort—or have thought I wanted that—but never to the degree that Jerry sacrificed his needs. In fact, my work has given him more freedom of choice, not less. Suddenly I feel very glad that he has never allowed me to dictate anything connected with the work part of his life.

He is both a better and a worse man than my father. He is troubled and unpredictable, secretive (I have now discovered)—and yet more brave. He has struggled so much harder, fought for his own life. He is meaner and crueler—but *he is not resigned.* He has not settled for less than all he can possibly have.

Somewhere along the line during these past weeks, I recall Jerry saying, "I just couldn't settle for despair." I wonder if that is what my father settled for. Without ever knowing it maybe. He never appears to be depressed; I can't ever recall thinking of him as sad. Suddenly that strikes me as very strange. How can you go through life never looking sad—unless you are only partly alive? He has settled for very meager fare. Jerry hasn't settled, and now I know he never will. He will struggle and fight for the most he can be—sexually, intellectually, emotionally—he wants everything—the most he can possibly have—and in that process he will hurt me—if I let him. Is it possible I can become more like him?

Would I really want to be a pet Pekingese, with temper tantrums, sitting on a satin pillow, petulant, demanding—owning another person? Something tells me it is not enough. It's even terrible. I wish I could just sit here and cry and be sorry for myself, but something is interfering. There is some part of me that is glad Jerry fought back against my enslavement. Some part of me knows that in the long run it will be *my* salvation. But I don't want to think about it—yet.

DREAM

Two days after writing the above, I had a dream. My mother and father were getting a divorce. At first I think it's some kind of terrible joke, but then I see they mean business. I am horrified, frightened, can't believe it. I hear them telling their friends that they are getting a divorce, and I yell at them that if this can happen to them, then marriage in general is finished—will never work for anyone.

My father says nothing, utterly passive. After much struggle, I finally get up enough courage to confront my mother, alone. We are in a restaurant in a lovely park. She begins to talk about how she has felt since she was a young girl: hemmed in by restrictions, over-protected, never having a chance to really live her own life. I can't believe what I am hearing—a real women's liberation speech. My mother begins to look younger and prettier; her face softens, her eyes glisten. I realize that what she is saying is probably true; it accounts for all her psychosomatic illnesses, her frustration, her anger. She tells me I have overidealized her relationship with my father. She was imprisoned by his passivity.

We walk out of the restaurant, and I realize that we are in Central Park at the restaurant that was once a barn for sheep, across from what is still called the Sheep Meadow. A little girl is looking over a low wall at the sheep; my mother has disappeared.

When I wake up, I write down the dream. It disturbs me. I wonder what Eve will say about it. I'm upset that my mother disappeared just as I seemed to be getting to know her for the first time—when I was seeing her as young and vulnerable—human. Where did the little girl come from? I remember watching those sheep myself as a child. Then I know: the dream is about me. The more I try to understand the ways in which I tried to copy my parents' marriage, the younger and prettier I will feel. If I will only listen to my own inner voices, I may even someday find the child I once was, who can probably teach me many things I need to understand. I feel triumphant; Eve couldn't have done a better job with this dream!

⌒ FIVE WEEKS

There is a part of me that really believes in Romeo and Juliet—in eternal love, in utter and complete fidelity for life —in romantic love—a kind of poetic part that has been really quite madly in love with one man all of my adult life. I cling with longing and pain and shock to the notion which I find quite beautiful, that two human beings can set themselves apart from everyone else in an intimacy that neither ever shares with anyone else—in friendship or passion—or even in anger.

And then there is another part of me—rational, insightful, psychologically sophisticated—that says it is nonsense for a man and a woman to deny themselves whatever rich variety of experience can add to the color of their short, mortal time—that recognizes that a good marriage can last fifty years and more, and that if one believes that all we've got, really, is the fullest use of all that we are and can be, and that nothing ought to be denied, then that is too long and too silly a time to require such utter devotion.

And yet—isn't that what I feel and want to give? In all these years I have never met a man as attractive, as interesting, as challenging, as the man I married. I simply cannot conceive of ever caring enough about anyone else to feel it would be worthwhile to wander. Ah, there's the anguish of it; the unshared feeling that this is the only possible intimacy for me—the loneliness of my centeredness.

The shock, when it hits me, is as fresh as that first black moment when I saw the letter that began "My Dearest Dear" and knew who it was from, and remembered that other moment, several years ago, when I saw them together on a street and felt I was the intruder, and had that hollow, agonizing wave of pain that filled the cavity of my whole being with terror—but I could never look at it. This time, there is no choice. I remember walking up and down, hiding in the bathroom, my knees shaking, a terrible chill all over, whispering, "Oh my God, Oh my God," and waiting for the children to leave—and hoping I would wake up—and knowing I would not—the first shock is *not* forgettable—I think I will recognize its special feeling for however much longer I may live, and it weighs me down, with a great burden that life is almost insupportable, no matter how good the good moments.

I know I am loved. We are closer. The attraction for me has never been stronger—and I think this is true for him, too. Sex has never been better. Why am I dying? Why does it seem that the Hoover Dam has less water in it than keeps pouring out of my eyes, day after day, long, long night after night?

The lies—the awful lies—that's the beginning of the pain. Two years—or was it even longer?—of not knowing such a big part of his life even existed. Where was I the first time they were together? What did he say when he came home? Was he elated and happy or distant and quiet? How did it happen, that first time? Was it sudden, did he moan and cry out, did it last long, did she rest her head in that hollow in his neck that I always called My Place? Did he want to get up right away and walk around? Did she make him fried eggs and bacon or a steak with onions? Do they talk afterward? Does she have an orgasm right away—or many? Does he breathe hard? Did he learn that new position from her? How soon after being with her was he ever with me—was it ever the same day or night? My God, I hope not the same day. Not to know—to be so cut off as not to know. And that's the puzzle—we are so close—or so it seemed to me. The dearest friend, the only confidante, the loved companion —how could I have not known his agony about the impotence? How could I have not known the inner passion— the need for more, the hunger for life, the unsatiated quest for fullness in life? Not to have sensed the degree of his inability to communicate—to have been so blind and smug and unaware that there was so much of that self that was never being shared with me, while I was sharing all. I thought we were communicating because *I* was—it seems quite incredible now.

But for all these months and years—the intimacy, oh my God, how I hate the body part—a lifetime of believing there is something basically unclean about sharing one's body with more than one's spouse. Did I give her a vaginal itch or did she give it to me? His tongue on her nipple, and in my mouth. Some microscopic part of her vaginal juices under the fingernail of the finger that touches me there. Does she kiss better? Does she take the Pill so that whenever they were together she could always be "ready"? There was certainly no chance that when they met it was to sleep from fatigue, or be busy with washing or cooking or burping and changing, or just coming home from the parent-teacher conference, or going to bed after trying to pay the bills without enough money to cover them in the bank.

The trouble with marriage is that it is daily living. Maybe it can't ever sustain that first marvelous hungry loving. Maybe the people who don't have affairs are settling for very little; maybe life can only be exciting when marriage doesn't interfere. And yet, and yet—here comes that wave of pain again—that hopeless, sad, deep nausea of my soul—if they met on a street corner, did he look at her with that sudden bright, all-over-the-face smile that warmed me so when we met at a theater or a restaurant? What was he thinking as each anniversary came around and he knew how little *I* knew about where we were with each other?

I remember the first week we were married, that whenever he came back to that ghastly room in the rooming house near the army post, there was a moment of such breathless cleaving to each other—a wild excitement in suddenly being able to put ourselves against each other and wrap our arms around each other, and *hold;* it was as if we were magnetized, and so drawn into each other's arms, that nothing could have stopped that movement. From the first moment of finding out I have wondered—is it like that, when they meet? I really do not believe that it is possible to share such a feeling with more than one person—it is impossible— and yet it seems to happen. I keep wondering when I will be able to live with such an idea, without suffering.

Four to six o'clock in the morning has become my worst time—that's what it is now. I try to think what they must have talked about. He says, with a self-righteousness that makes me want to kill him, that he never even mentioned me. Did he talk about his work? Does he ask her advice as he does mine? What else do we talk about that he might share with her? I can't think of any subject that doesn't belong to us—our work, our daughter, and us. Does he talk about his childhood, his therapy? His *suffering*? Could he tell *her*?

Who is she? I think she was small and dark and wore glasses. I remember on the street, in that terrible moment of knowledge, that I comforted myself with the thought that she was not glamorous. He will tell me nothing—and I guess that is why I play these games with myself. Let me say it—what I think she must be. Quiet, probably, a less demanding person, with less of a passion for life. Quite helpless, dependent—someone who needs his counsel, a person who needed someone to lean on, and who did not ask for very much. No conditions like marriage or "Leave your wife," or "Love me only," or "See me often," or maybe not even forcing him to say "I love you." Maybe not even that. Poor, poor girl. I think from the little I saw of that letter, she really cares. I think she might be a mixed-up, less competent person than I—I know she's changed professions many times and had other lovers—and maybe leads quite an unhappy life.

She took so little; in all this time there could not have been many times together for more than a few hours. I wonder now about those trips I had to take—were those the time they could spend the night together? Could he have been with her when he called me to wish me luck or ask how my work was going? What would I do if I were her? If I could only have a moment, here or there, and none of the safety or permanence of the friendship we have—I really believe—for all our married life? I guess then I would really die. What has happened to her since I found out? With the drowning and the storm and the pain and the great moments of trying to reach each other in new ways—is she more sensitive to change than I was? Can she read him better than I did, after all these years of marriage? He has shared my turmoil and agony, and he has certainly not been spending much time away from me. How did he explain this sudden preoccupation with home and family? How the fatigue, when I guess she was expecting an eager and loving return from our trip? Is he having awful scenes with her, too? Is she afraid of losing him? Or is she so saintlike (and if so, what's wrong with her?) that she just accepts whatever crumbs are now available? Am I still naive and insensitive, incapable of looking at his capacity to leave me out and away—is it possible she knows nothing, sees no change, that somehow he is finding time—during the day perhaps? How dear he has tried to be about not going to evening meetings! For, of course, that's how it was done.

I think back to the average evening of the past two years. Almost never home before nine or ten, most often too tired to talk to me. Ever since Julie left—the feeling that we almost never met to be together—no suppertime any more. What did we do on weekends? Rarely saw friends any more—isolated ourselves—I thought it was our work and wanting to be alone together. What did we do? I have gone to the theater and movies alone most of the time these past few years. I spent a lot of time alone. As I look back now, I see there was a chasm, a separateness—often covered by affection and genuine enjoyment of each other's company—but I see now that only a piece of him was there with me; it was never whole.

Has it been whole this past month? Am I still living with

illusions, with pushing away what I don't want to see? It has seemed like a new falling in love—a standing naked in a way we never dared before, with our souls quivering in the cold air, but staying there, feeling the danger and the chill, but not going away. It has seemed like a reaching and a touching and a never-again-deceiving kind of time—and yet, and yet—I am afraid to trust it. I see a dark head on the pillow next to him, and it is not mine. I walk along a street, and suddenly there is the image of a smaller girl reaching up to kiss him on the lips—I see a private smile in their eyes. I wonder what secret jokes there are for their love-making—and none of the new closeness seems real or possible. When you are falling in love, shouldn't there just be two, even at that time? Maybe not all the years of marriage—but at least for falling in love? And isn't that what it is now? Maybe falling in love better—with some greater knowledge that one cannot make conditions or promise anything for tomorrow, but can only exult in the moment of loving.

I would love him and want to be with him, I guess, even if the affair goes on forever. I cannot believe this is true, and I wonder if it is my depravity or my strength.

Is she funny? Does he make her his "little girl"? Do they have a special language with each other? Why can't I endure that there might be all this intimacy and privacy without me? Is it absolutely true and proven that I am wrong to feel this way?

I wonder if she's interesting. Does she give him ideas for his work? Is she part of some of the ideas he's been working on these past few years? Has he given her presents? What were they? Jewelry? I wonder how often; and if he hasn't, what is the limit of her ability to give without wanting anything to be given? Is his need of her all that she requires? Is his need of me all that I require? Yes—that's easy to answer—

it really is—and I guess my trouble is that my idea of needing is all-inclusive—a need for no one else. It is demanding
the superhuman of myself and of him—and yet it seems
right. I learned to believe this when I was so young—probably by the time I was five or six—and even after all these
years of therapy, I wonder if you ever really change that five-
year-old's view of what is right and wrong? I guess I really
have, on other issues—maybe, maybe, if I can—if the pain
would just stop, if I only didn't wake up crying in the night
—if only I did not think of her. Could I ever learn to really
let go? To be glad for whatever there is, with whatever person, in whatever place, that enriches his experience? Could
I ever do that? I cannot believe it is possible, and yet I know
that this is what I must try to do.

Part of me believes in romantic love and fidelity in marriage, and that it would be impossible, where two people
really love each other, for one to deceive the other for any
length of time. I was discussing that with a friend at the
beach last summer—that neither of us could imagine that a
loving wife would not know. Jerry was in New York, and
perhaps with her, when my friend and I agreed about this
on the beach.

Part of me now knows that I am a child, that I make
dreams, that I deny unhappiness. That if he was as unhappy
as he says he was, then there was something wrong with me
in not perceiving it, in thinking he was making the same
compromises with life that I was making—that work and
genuine affection and friendship were so much, that if sex
was infrequent and uncertain, that was a small price to pay
for all else. No compromise at all for him—he was stretching
himself and searching, and taking chances, and investing in
another person's life—all without my knowing. *That* is what
I don't want to look at. Could it be that her image appears,

over and over again, to keep me from having to look at myself? My failures in marriage? My assumptions, my smugness, my looking away?

But there were always such good times, such special times —gentleness and understanding, such encouragement for my work, and such a feeling of wonder on my part that, despite one area of difficulty, that this marvelous and handsome man was married to me. "One area of difficulty"—what a copout! Nicely sealed off as a minor matter—when, in truth, of course, it was a civilized man's only outcry against being owned. Never leaving me, never making me feel unworthy as a human being, never able to tell me how often he felt trapped by my needs and demands—probably frightened half to death (and consumed by anger) that I was going to be as demanding and unhappy as my mother—unable to tell me how he suffered—and yet there for me, in so many ways.

Is it possible I can stop thinking about that other woman in his arms, if I think about him? Or about what we need to do about us? No, it won't be as simple and well organized as that. Everything we are living and learning right now will help, but I think I must first accept the part of me that wants to be the only one; I have to put up with my obsessions, my jealousy and rage, my puritanical shock, the agony of thinking about them together. Long as it's taking, it can't be stopped or put off, I have to go on with it, no matter how desolate nights or sudden sharp aching afternoons it may take. I have to go on with it—the Other Woman theme. It's got to drain out of me.

Somewhere in me I think there may be another person starting to grow. I hate it now, and I am not really ready to even look at it, but I think it is what makes it possible for me to love now, more than ever before. Some tiny, tiny voice, somewhere dim and ghostlike, that wants to affirm

life, take each moment and glory in it, alone, love freely and
without price of any kind—just because the love must be and
I can't stop it from coming. Loving without conditions, laws,
regulations, loving without exclusivity, if necessary, opening
to life as fully as I seem to have opened to sex these past few
weeks. Ah, yes, it's that openness I seek—not in the act of
sex but in the act of being alive. I cannot imagine it, and
yet if I can write that I cannot imagine it, I am already imagining it. But I wonder, can there still be times when it
will be us two, alone? Some moments, some months? I know
I will move where I have to move—to no rules—but without
rules, could it still be us alone, sometimes?

I feel quiet inside. I had a dream about wanting to be
"beautiful and good." I woke up thinking about Julie; she
has become that for me. She is so open and natural. It's
strange that I feel this way, because she has almost been
angrier about Jerry's affair than I.

She brought the subject up last time she was here. We
were in the kitchen, alone together. She said, "Mom, I know
what you have been going through, and I could kill Daddy."
I thought I'd been so good at concealing it. "Are you nuts?"
she said. "I knew from the beginning. Nothing else could
have made you look so *crumbled*. Andy and I talked about
it a lot. Daddy is a rat."

I couldn't understand this at all. Julie has had a number
of relationships, all loving and monogamous, but successive.
I would have thought she would side with Jerry and feel
that I was childish. It is so strange (and kind of wonderful!)
to find her taking my part—obviously not out of any in-
tellectual or rational conviction, but simply because she loves
me and doesn't like seeing my suffering. What a gift she is!
Her adolescence was so stormy and rebellious—so terrifying
to me—that I can barely believe that this lovely young

woman, who cares so much about me, can be that same un-happy child.

How strange to be talking to my daughter as a confidante, an understanding woman! She tells me that her theory is that Jerry needed someone more like himself. "Daddy has a very limited ability to give,' to communicate; I think he probably wanted a relationship that would demand much less of him than you do. She's probably a quiet, inhibited girl who leans on him a lot. You're so *forceful*. I understand how Daddy feels. Now that I live away from home, I really enjoy your blustery-ness, your earthy, noisy, openness. But it drove me crazy when I was younger. Daddy and I are more reserved, scared of a lot of emotion. My guess is that the other relationship is much less intense on every level."

At first I am very uneasy talking about all this with my own child. It seems very disloyal to Jerry—and I don't want Julie to stop loving her father. He was wonderful to her during the difficult years, and she adored him. At that time she couldn't stand the sight of me! Julie puts me at ease. "Don't worry. I'm so mad I could kill him, but I understand him. I always knew you were the strong one, he was really the weak one. I knew that you really took care of all of us. He's a little crazy—but that's OK."

Then Julie says something that startles me completely—sets a whole new feeling, a new perspective in motion. She says, "You know, you could survive if Daddy left you—but he would come apart at the seams if you ever left him; he'd be finished."

✐ SIX WEEKS

DIALOGUE

ME: It seems absolutely impossible for me to imagine sleeping with two people; what happens if you think of one when you are with the other one? How do you remember which private words and actions belong where? Being in love means one person to me. . . .

JERRY: There are different levels of love, different kinds. [*It is clear he won't tell me if he ever thought of her when he was with me, or vice versa. Any questions about her make him terribly uncomfortable. I guess she never asked about me.*]

ME: I feel so ashamed, just knowing that *she* knew you were unfaithful to me. She must have thought I had failed you, that I'm no good. . . .

JERRY: I don't know what she thinks, and we never, ever mentioned you, but her background is European, and I am sure her attitude is very different from yours. I'm sure she assumes this is a normal occurrence even in the best of marriages. . . .

ME: That makes me sick. I don't understand that feeling at all. I could never, ever love anyone else unless you died or we got a divorce and I stopped loving you. One love would have to be over before I could start loving someone else. It's just too personal, too intimate, too private. It's being the most special person in the whole world to someone else. . . .

JERRY: You are the most special person to me; you matter

more than anyone else. As the central person in my life, I want to be with you. . . .

ME: Suppose something terrible happened—like we got bombed, or there was a terrible epidemic, or there was no more food or water—even if you stayed with me, wouldn't you worry about her and want to help her?

JERRY: Yes, I would always want to help her if I could, but I consider my relationship to you the most important in my life.

ME: Gee—thanks for small favors. [*Jerry's face closes. I feel myself getting panicky. I can't stop asking dumb, questions.*] What would you expect me to do if you died? Would she come to the funeral? Would you expect me to endure that? Suppose it was the other way around and I had a lover and he came to my funeral— what would you do?

JERRY: I hope I would go and comfort him—and thank him if he had made you happy and given you something I couldn't.

ME: My God, how noble! You're not *human!* If you really loved me as much as you say you do, you'd be jealous, you'd want to *kill,* you'd feel as murderous as I do toward Nina. . . .

JERRY: That's your idea about love. It isn't mine.

ME: Maybe we can never understand each other again. God, I wish I were dead.

⌒ TWO MONTHS

I am sitting on the window seat, fourteen floors above the street. It is almost dusk, and I am fascinated by a kind of *pull* inside me—like a strong wind going through me, urging me to open the window and let myself fall out. How long would I be conscious? If only I knew it would be over before I hit the ground—that it wouldn't hurt. I'm such a coward about pain. It seems absurd—even immoral!—that I'm more afraid to die painfully than to live in the agony I now feel.

I sit here writing, knowing that beyond my anguish is FURY! If I fell out the window, it would destroy Jerry's life forever. That is the perfect revenge. Sleeping with another man, leaving him, shaming him in some way—hanging on to him in the helpless dependence as I guess I've been doing—these are all child's play compared to making him live with my suicide! My God, how I wish I could do it! I want him to suffer, terribly, and nothing could possibly accomplish this goal more perfectly.

I let the rage surge through me. I become less and less fascinated with the idea of falling, of seeing what it feels like when you defy the laws of gravity. I become more and more preoccupied with my anger—and then, after it shakes me for a few minutes, I find it fading. Can you *really* hate someone you love and need so much, that you could want him to live in such a hell all the rest of his life? It horrifies me that I could have such feelings, but I will not let them go—I have to face them. Half of me just doesn't want to live any more, and half of me wants to hurt Jerry beyond measure; now what is it that keeps me here, unable to open the window, using writing as a way to keep me sitting here?

My statistics must be wrong! That's the story of my life—failing mathematics! Let me try to face all of it. Maybe 10 percent longs for the surcease of pain enough to want a final sleep; maybe another 15 percent would like to torture Jerry. But I *think* that leaves 75 percent of something else—what is it? I find that it was easier to be honest about the neurotic feelings. I can tell that what I am about to write is positive, and I don't want to admit that there can be healthy strivings in me, when I feel so bruised. But write it, Jo—you know already what it is; it is *loving and wonder.* I love Jerry, I love life—I might even someday love myself! And the truth is that, despite everything that has happened, I am still full of wonder about the future; I want to know how it will all come out! Will we stay together? Will we love each other— maybe even more? Someday might I even become a good enough writer to write this story? Could I ever get enough distance from it to be able to look at it, to see it in perspective? And what will we become that we aren't yet?

It is dark outside now. Jerry was so explicit over the phone, exactly where he will be this evening and for how long. Is it to be kind and to comfort me that he is not going to see Nina? Or is he covering his tracks as he's been doing for two years? Now come the waves of pain—more tears. I wonder how much crying a human being's eyes can stand. I am certainly finding out. I am through with the window. I begin to feel small, shriveled, a little child, scared, alone, un- loved. Shall I pull myself together, wear dark glasses, go for a long walk, so I can sleep—or shall I curl up in my bed and give in? To bed.

I dreamed of a confrontation between Nina and me. But it was hazy and dim and I couldn't hear what we were say- ing to each other. Eve said, "Well, go on with the dream— make up a dialogue with Nina."

DIALOGUE (*A Fantasy*)

ME: I have often wondered if I would ever have the guts to kill another human being—whether I could shoot someone, even to save my own life. I look at you with such rage and such loathing, and I know that if I had a gun I would not hesitate for a moment to kill you. I would only be sorry that you would die with too little pain. I would rather have the strength to strangle you with my bare hands, or poke your eyes out, or burn you very slowly. . . .

NINA: I get the point—you couldn't make it any clearer.

ME: I have just told you that I know you are having an affair with my husband, and you haven't batted an eye; you seem calm and collected and quite comfortable.

NINA: What do you think I should do? Get down on my knees and beg your forgiveness? Who are you to claim such ownership? Did you buy him at a slave market? Jerry is an enormously attractive man, as you surely know; I find it quite unbelievable that I am the only mistress he has had.

ME: That word makes me sick to my stomach; I just cannot bear it. I cannot be part of his harem—it makes me nothing—a thing of no value, no importance. . . .

NINA: I find you one of the strangest creatures I have ever met. He has stayed married to you for all of his adult life, he doesn't want to leave you, he is capable of loving you more and better than ever before; he is with you almost all of the time he is not working—and *you* feel like a nothing! What would that make me, if I operated by your standards? A flea! Do you have any idea how quickly and gladly I would change places with you? If I could have the love and protection and respect that you have, I would never give it a thought if Jerry had ten mistresses. . . .

ME: If you feel that way, why do you look so contented, unruffled, at ease, in a situation that seems so unendurable to me?

NINA: I really can't explain that to you. I don't know why. Maybe I don't value myself as highly as you do yourself. Maybe it never occurs to me that I must have more than conditional love. Maybe you have always had more, so you demand more. Then again, it is also possible that I respect myself so much that I do not need other people to give me proof of how much they care for me; I take what pleasure I can in a relationship, and am philosophical about it. Of course, one thing is certain—and in this, I feel only sorry for you—I was not raised to have the ridiculous notions of fidelity that you have. I did not think a married woman was less of a person because her husband was unfaithful; it always seemed a natural thing for men and women in Europe. I can see you are a victim of very bad training.

ME: Good or bad depends on your viewpoint. I have tried desperately to change this opinion, and yet I always come back to it; I find something quite beautiful and inspiring in the idea of marital fidelity—I just can't help it. You're right—I was taught too early—and now having tried so hard to change, for the two longest and most terrible months of my life, I feel I just cannot change. I feel as if I have been sinning in living with Jerry, knowing he had another woman. I also find a sense of revulsion at the thought of his making love to someone else during the same weeks—my God, maybe even the same days—as with me. It sickens me to such a degree that I really long for the oblivion of dying. But most of all, I feel like half a woman. I think about the women I know whose husbands would never wander, except perhaps in occasional fantasy—and I wonder—are they so much more attractive and interesting than I am? I can't quite manage it. I still feel I must have failed in some way. All my married life I have felt a failure, inadequate, incapable of getting a man's full love—and I never knew what that did to Jerry.

NINA: You are a very greedy person, at the same time that you think so little of yourself. Perhaps these things go together. You are really a very complicated person. I see that with you, Jerry could never be bored! You are full of contradictions. The more you talk, the more I feel myself to be less complicated. . . .

ME: I don't think so at all; I find your acceptance of what will be, utterly mysterious and quite unbelievable—if it is real. After all, I made you up, and that sure as hell doesn't satisfy my curiosity about the real person. I have imagined you into a woman who would give Jerry pleasure with no complications—but I wonder if that is true; from a word or two lately, I have the impression things are not running so smoothly between you. Now I wonder if you cry and carry on as I do.

NINA: Maybe what you have not considered as a possibility is that you are not all one thing, and neither am I. Maybe in you there is the unused capacity to give freely, without demanding—and maybe in me, there is some of the suffering you have experienced. No one is all one thing or another.

ME: I wanted to meet you to tell you that I can't go on as things are. It is just destroying me to live and love a man who has a girl friend on the side. I am too ashamed and disgusted by it. I have just about decided that we will have to separate.

NINA: I am delighted to hear it. Then he and I will have more time together, and he will be less distracted and guilt-laden—as he has seemed to be lately. The question is, which of us loves him more? You, who have to have everything, or I, who can settle for whatever he wants to give me, and can be glad I make him happy—even if there are times when it pains me, just as it does you?

ME: It isn't only how much one loves him, but also how much one loves oneself. If I behave in ways that are utterly alien to myself, then I can't stand myself.

NINA: I have the feeling that your problem is that you won't accept the fact that you can have two feelings simultaneously—that you can want to give and make him happy, and that at the very same time you can suffer terribly because he sometimes turns to me.

ME: I can't live with both feelings—I have tried desperately for two months.

NINA: Then the only thing to do is to live alone. . . .

ME: That would be even worse.

NINA: I am sorry for you, but I can't help you.

What a naive child I seem to have been! By this time, a few close friends know what has happened. A week or so after I found out about Nina, Evelyn called; just suddenly, out of the blue. We hadn't talked to each other for half a year, I guess. She said she'd been thinking about me a lot and felt uneasy—had the feeling something was the matter. At first I tried to hide it, but we have been such close friends since childhood, and I was so relieved to hear her voice and hear the love in it. I finally burst out crying and told her what had happened. We talked for a long time, and I kept repeating that the worst part of all was the lying, and the fact that it was impossible for me to imagine how anyone could love two people at the same time. She was compassionate and loving at first, and then I began to sense some hesitancy in her reactions—as if she was thinking her own thought and was retreating in some ways.

DIALOGUE

ME: Are you disgusted with me? Do I sound like a helpless idiot?

EVELYN: No, darling, not at all. I hear the hurt and I am really suffering with you. . . .

ME: I hear a "but." . . .

EVELYN: Jo—NOBODY knows this—I want to tell you, but it scares me. I don't know how you will react. Eve is right; you *can* love two people at the same time. I do. . . .

ME: WHAT? I don't believe it. My God, you and Richard . . .

EVELYN: I still love him. I don't want to leave him. I live in terror, but there is someone else. There has been for three years. I just couldn't tell you when you were here, but I was dying of loneliness. I need you to understand. Maybe now we can help each other.

ME: If you *and* Eve tell me it is possible, I think I will have to begin to believe it. I love you and respect you so profoundly. What has happened? Does Richard really not know? Doesn't lying hurt your marriage?

EVELYN: Of course it does. It is agony. I want to tell Richard, but it would kill him. He would never accept it. And I don't want to lose him.

ME: I can't believe I am really having this conversation with you. I must be having a nightmare.

EVELYN: Jo, don't make me sorry I told you. I'm trying to give you a gift. It is dangerous and frightening for me to tell you. I want to try to help you understand it can happen. . . .

We talk for almost an hour; then there are long, long letters, and more phone calls. Eventually we manage to see each other. I begin to see that there have been pieces missing in Evelyn's marriage and in her life. Richard is a clinger, like me; he wants to own her. He has been jealous of her talent, her success. He wants her to be the devoted, understanding wife who is more interested in his work than in her own.

An accident of fate—a sudden meeting with a giant of a human being—a man bound and gagged in a terrible marriage from which he is struggling to escape. At first they talk about their problems, their children—and then, slowly, it seems that what each has to offer the other is a passionate direction, a demand, "Be yourself! Don't sell out!" Both suffer terribly because of the dishonesty; they separate from each other many times. But I learn that Evelyn's marriage is far better when she allows herself the second relationship; it founders terribly when she tries to deny it to herself. I begin to wonder what might happen if Richard were told and were able to tolerate it—allow it. *And what about me?* I feel so torn. I love Evelyn and am so deeply touched that she has confided in me in order to try to help me. On the other hand, she and Richard have been married even longer than Jerry and I, and I can't help but identify with Richard. He and I are the offended parties. I struggle terribly—especially after I see Evelyn and recognize how much she is suffering. She is in great pain, but there is much more to it than that. I also have to acknowledge that she is more alive, more exciting—more womanly—than ever before.

Another friend I confided in laughed at me! We were at a conference together, sharing a room. She kept asking me what was the matter—I seemed so much more subdued, and I moaned in my sleep at night.

DIALOGUE

ME: Well, Jerry and I have been having some problems. It's not exactly marriage on the rocks, but it seemed that way for a while. . . .

EDITH: You mean you don't love each other any more?

ME: No, nothing like that. I found out he was having an affair.

EDITH: [*laughs!*] Oh, Jo, I thought it was something really serious! My God, you are such a little prude! Listen— a lot of people tell me their troubles, and I know a lot of married people, and I swear, I do not know one single couple where this hasn't happened to one or the other, sooner or later. . . .

ME: *I* know lots of couples where it doesn't happen. . . .

EDITH: That's what *you* think! You're just gullible. . . .

ME: That's not true. I do know some couples who absolutely adore each other and couldn't possibly look at anyone else. . . .

EDITH: Yeah—and what are they like? Be honest! Aren't they among the dullest people you know?

ME: They're very nice, good people. . . .

EDITH: JO! Don't they bore you a little?

ME: I take "The Fifth"!

A new thing to think about: Can it be possible that smooth sailing in a marriage costs a price? That somehow both partners make an unconscious pact not to rock the boat? Does that make them less interesing people? Does it block some kind of richness of experience, personality, talent? It is one of the blackest of thoughts and I don't believe it. I have always believed the exact opposite: that love can only make a person more fulfilled. When Edith and I talk again a few months later, I tell her she really shook me up. We argue some more. Her final comment is, "I think the problem is that we don't have the same definition of love." I ask what she means, and she holds her hand out, palm open. "Love is having a beautiful butterfly light on your hand and never touching it; watching it, seeing its beauty, wanting to keep it forever—but knowing that if you try to hold onto it, you will kill it."

As time passes and the initial shock and shame lessen (what a surprise that this happens!), I have confided in one or two other friends—and the reaction is always the same:

1. You're damned lucky if it's only happened once!
2. You—and everybody else I know!
3. Most marriages survive this—if they are good enough to last in the first place.
4. It's really not such a terrible thing; you're over-reacting.

I'm trying to think of anyone who was shocked and horrified. Then I realize that of course I would never confide in someone like that; I have very carefully chosen as confidantes those who I know will be more broad-minded, more open, more experienced in such matters.

But the truth is that when I think over the general array of our close friends and try to imagine how they would react, it seems to me that very few of them would be horrified. Something is happening to *me*—that's really what it's all about. The day I found out, I could not have told anyone, and I would have felt sure they would have been as shocked as I was. Now I see that I was projecting my own attitudes onto other people. This thought makes me feel a little more grown up. I am learning and changing—I can feel it.

It suddenly occurs to me that I have shared this period of my life with only one man friend—and he because he is married to a friend, and I write to both of them. As I begin to think about it, I realize that *he* was the greatest comfort of all, even though my women friends were more available more of the time. I have found a letter he wrote to me. It starts, "I have the most powerful urge to envelop you in a hug of great affection, protection and comfort. . . . Please know that a certain gentleman—me—loves you very, very knowingly, and if you were here would probably be squeezing you breathless. . . ."

I felt so attacked as a woman, and those words helped to put those pieces of me back together again.

The issue of "disclosure" is shifting. At first I felt as if I were sharing the worst secret in the world. Then I discovered that my secret was not exactly original. Now I sometimes have the feeling that a time might come when I would not mind letting anyone know. Come to think of it, if it were not for all the peripheral people who could still be hurt or embarrassed, I think a time might come when I could even let people read this diary! Am I going crazy or getting sane?

⌒ *EIGHT DAYS ON A BOAT*

Day Two:

This is our first vacation together since our troubles began. It is agonizing. At home I rarely do anything to hide how I am feeling. Here, on this cruise ship, seeing Jerry so happy and relaxed, I just can't let him know how miserable I feel.

For some reason I don't understand, I am once again

totally preoccupied with Nina. Everytime I see Jerry staring out at the sea, I wonder if he is thinking about her. Does he miss her? Does he wish he had taken a trip like this with her? Jerry is very amorous; I can't really respond. I've been pretending. Girls are so lucky they can get away with that! Poor men, never to be able to feign sexual enthusiasm. Eve feels pretending is as damaging to a marriage as infidelity. In any event, I think women—especially the more radical women's liberationists—greatly underestimate how much more threatened men are by this physiological difference.

I lie in bed, again imagining Jerry and Nina making love. As soon as I am sure that Jerry is asleep, I cry and cry. I thought I was so much better—but I suppose what's happening is that all our other boat trips were so different—so innocent. We were inviolate, unattackable, could not be permeated by any outsiders. Now all that has changed. It will never be the same again. And having to keep quiet about how I am feeling is so much harder than giving in to my feelings. Maybe that's progress. For the first time I am really considering Jerry's needs and feelings; I just can't spoil this time for him. On the other hand, am I being too deceitful? Won't that poison our relationship all over again?

I keep thinking of how we used to pretend that *we* were having an affair, on the first couple of trips we took to Europe by boat. We were running away from feeling married. One part of me feels it was very romantic and that nothing as good as that can ever happen again. But there is another part of me that is having thoughts I don't want to think about: memories of sexual difficulties on some of those trips; other times in other places where I didn't tell Jerry how miserable I was feeling.

I think that any place or time where you are *supposed* to be having a wonderful time is difficult to endure! Vacations are really hard on people. At home, with all the ordinary miseries of daily rout:nes, problems, realities, nobody has to be cheerful or happy all the time. When you are spending a fortune on *having* a good time, you feel a sense of obligation about it. It's the same thing that happens on holidays. It is the gritted-teeth-pleasure syndrome!

Day Four:
After writing the above, I decided it was wrong to pretend. After lunch today, we came back to the cabin to take a nap. Jerry started making love to me, and instead of pretending to enjoy it, I burst into tears. I told him how I'd been feeling. He was genuinely shocked and terribly sad. He'd been so happy, thought everything was so good between us. When I saw him draw away, go into his shell, I could have killed myself for not keeping up the game. Now I have ruined the trip for both of us.

Day Five:
Yesterday and today have been awful. Jerry says he just feels utterly discouraged. Nothing he does comes out right. I tell him that I wish I'd kept on pretending. He says no, that would not have been right. But now he feels the way he always used to feel: that no matter what he tried to do for me it was never enough, never made me happy. Suddenly I realized both of us are reacting in old ways to a new situation. This time I am *not* demanding anything from him; I only want to try to be real, not fool him. He is very thoughtful when I say this. "You may be right," he says. "The trouble is that whenever you are not happy, I immediately blame myself. That's the feeling of despair I tried to explain to you."

"I don't blame you for my feeling unhappy on this trip,"

I tell him. "I don't want to be the kind of person who is obsessed with the past, can't give myself to available pleasures in the present. I just don't want to be a fake with you. I want both of us to try to be more real with each other."

Day Eight:
The last two days of the trip have been altogether different. The air is cleared; there is both pain and pleasure for both of us—we are accepting the package deal.

∽ FIVE MONTHS

I need to go back—I have to go back—and look at where I've been, what Jerry and I are made of—our beginnings with each other. It is as if the only solace I will be able to find is if I can *understand*—see the things I missed or brushed away. When I am not visualizing Jerry and Nina in bed together, my mind is full of scenes of our past—trying to fit pieces of a puzzle together. It is as if the pieces never quite fit before, but I never cared or bothered; now it is absolutely essential that I find the right piece for the right place.

When I tell Eve about this, she gently suggests that one way to do this is to study my perceptions of Jerry since we first met. She has learned by now that some of the best help she can give me is to encourage me to explore through writing—that this has become far more than catharsis in these past few months.

On my way out of her office I suddenly say, "I have a title for a story about Jerry; it will be, 'The Always Hidden Man.'" I take a taxi home instead of walking—I can't wait to begin it.

THE ALWAYS HIDDEN MAN

In the very beginning . . .

A flirt—very, very sexy and attractive—somehow bolder with me than any other boy in a long while—unwilling to accept my wall of self-protection, seeming to see *me* as lusty as I saw him. Naughty and very nice . . . kind of crazy letters; then, after the first meeting, full of passionate propositioning!

The most interesting and fascinating boy I'd ever met, very sensual, I felt an attraction I had never felt before. Saw him as wild and free, but also gentle and kind and very dear. Utterly remote about his beginnings—for some time had no idea whether or not he even had a family, who they were— this seemed to be something from which he'd totally separated himself—it no longer existed in his experiencing of life. . . . Was all this wish to stay with me, to sleep with me —was that special or for many girls? He said nothing that could suggest it was special—except he wanted to. I only understood that there was SOMETHING quite unusual and terribly important happening between us, and because I was an emotional infant, I saw that maybe I was falling in love, but had no idea what he was feeling—and only hoped it would be love, and that *he would want to marry me*; my whole life was focused on that one reality.

In the falling in love . . .

Great gentleness with me—never pushing, a complete acceptance of the rigid, puritanical limits I set on lovemaking —but I believed that there was great sensuality in me and that if I was a good girl, and got him to marry me, my rewards for having been so good and pure until the right moment would be very great, indeed. Much wonderful talk about ideas and work and plans—but, looking back, it seems to me I already sensed areas of remoteness, of unconnectedness. Now he lists his family, but still without any feeling or relatedness. I meet some of his family, finally, and cannot see how or where there could be a relation to such people. They seem cold and coarse and dull; I am extremely uneasy with them.

I know Jerry does not want marriage (and can see why!), but I'm so sure I know best, and there will be no regrets because it will be the affair he wants, but on my terms. Everyone in my life agreed with that principle; men never want to marry—but if you hold out, they will, and then you can let it be what they wanted in the first place.

And so they were married . . .
Everything I expected—passion, a hunger, a reaching and clutching, a touching, a being with another person, in a way I never had been and only barely imagined. The wonder and delights of the body—the awakening of feelings *never, never* permitted through before—the exhilaration, the exultation to discover what I could feel—the pride and joy—all shared and understood, all delighted in, all encouraged. Tenderness and passion and fun and giggling, and holding, and playing, and talking, endless talking—it seemed at the time that we unfolded to each other utterly, but . . .

Then came the time to live together, to have a home . . .
Fear begins. Shame, all the old terrors of not being attractive enough, I suppose, looking back, some secret sense that I *was* a brazen oversexed hussy, just as I must have feared during all those years of careful suppression. The turning away, the "I'm so tired," the "Hard day in the army," and finally the "back trouble." All nicely covered, not talked about except

as valid reasons. I seemed never to have even heard about impotence and the thought that there could be such a thing in this man who had pursued me so aggressively (or so I naively thought—in truth, he let me set the pace all along). The nights of crying and walking, of sitting at the living room window, the terror, what did it mean? Where did it come from? The first frightening talks about what made him who he was, the absence of memory, the terror of looking within, the totally cut off feeling about family and child-hood—and when we finally began to talk about the impotence as a thing having its own reality, that strange moment when, lying in bed, he said, when we talked of therapy, "I know that if I look into a mirror, I will see something terribly evil, a horror."

The long walks, the black moods, a beginning, creeping awareness of the deep, dark complexities of this man, so kind and gentle, so accommodating to me, so loving—with some dark places of the soul, and in some way deeply broken and split inside. The growing agony of seeing, for both of us, my wanting to believe that he'd been somehow greatly damaged in childhood, but knowing that what I *really* thought was that I was unattractive.

No family time . . .
The tree outside the living room window, the endless nights of weeping—winter—always winter and snow. A man disappearing, unknown—and yet, always, from the beginning on, those other times, the reaching out, the needing and the touching, the sharing of worries and problems and work experiences, the friends who loved to visit our "marvelous nest," the pleasure in my homemaking and cooking, the pride in my achievements—always the support, always the love—and always the anguish, too. Was the impotence part of not

wanting children? The trying to believe that his fear of children was another sign of early psychic wounding—but my inner belief that no one could really love me; I was responsible.

He expresses absolute terror of having a child; he doesn't know why—but feels it. Yet he buys me a Teddy bear one Christmas and makes it a live thing—leaves me notes, signed "Teddy." Funny, dear—utterly childlike. I would find Teddy sitting on the toilet, or on the pillow, or at the kitchen table. How long did he write me notes?

Things go from bad to worse. After three years of marriage, a real psychological breakdown. A man who now seemed twisted and badly wounded, failing in marriage, failing in work. And yet, despite that, the *rock* to which I clung, the source of all my strength, the greatest need, the greatest source of comfort—the person to whom I ran for solace and understanding and encouragement. The source of all the pain and all the joy—there never has been any other way, and now it seems quite wondrous and strange; the never turning away, the never abandoning, on either side; the depths of despair endured, and always followed, sooner or later, by a marvelous closeness; and always the fun, too! But the agony of the time of life when all my friends began to be pregnant and have babies; the anger and the fear in him, and did I also begin to sense some hatred, which I was never able to acknowledge? It seems so now. The weeping for sex, the weeping for a baby, the weeping for that boy I'd known in the first months of our meeting, and the weeping most of all, I guess, for my failure, my lack, my somewhere ugly self that must have been responsible.

And all the years . . .

Things seeming to be better, I thought, with some therapy

here and there. On the surface we seemed happy—we had many friends, did a lot of entertaining, moved ahead in our work, learned a lot, and sometimes enjoyed our lives. There was a lot of love underneath the fears and tension, but also the pain, the periods of sexual frustration, the long, dark walks, the loss of contact—and then, always, and just as real, the fun of being away alone together—the first trip to Europe, that moment of closing a hotel door and reaching to each other with such hunger and longing, the affection and the help—the helping me in my work, the sharing the care of Julie when we finally had the child *I* wanted, the pride in our homes and what I did with them, the boasting of my work, the encouragement, the strong, clear, "Go girl, go," every inch of the way.

And yet, did I ever stop to look or really listen? Did I ever sense the real anguish that I've since learned was there? Could I have? Did he ever let it show in any way except in sex and in not wanting children? Were there messages that I couldn't pick up? I cannot recall any words telling me how awful it was for him—it was his inability to say, and my great *competence* in handling life, that shut us both off from his pain.

The years and the years and the years of good therapy, and growing, the feeling, for me, of having such companionship, such friendship, such understanding, the wanting to let me be and become. How I talked and talked and talked, and said all my feelings, and complained and complained about the little things, the wanting more, the deep discontent of something missing, but never knowing what, and of understanding so little of the burdens of need I imposed, and of my inner hunger for something unprovided. Telling every feeling and every thought must have been the reassurance, the constantly needed reassurance that everything was fine for us. The stormy confrontations about sex, the explosions of our agony, the slowly building acceptance; there will be high times when we are alone; all we have to do is be rid of the responsibility of Julie and go away alone and then we can have everything; the times that disproved this, that I couldn't look at; the summertimes when she was at camp, when nothing really changed at all. The beginnings of acceptance and covering; the beginning of not sharing every feeling about sex; the beginning of pretending to be OK without it, for long periods of time, the closing of myself, the denial of feelings, the desexualizing of my energies—all this is clear in memory—but the *man?* An awareness that *I never really knew anything about the toll it was taking.*

The final explanation and resignation . . .
This is a man who might have been a monk at one time; this is a man who cerebralized his libido, out of the agony of childhood; at least he saved his marvelous mind. His *work,* that is the core of his being; my jealousy of it—and also my pride in his achievements, the growing awareness of the true brilliance of that mind—and the guilt that I interfered with it, with my demands that he be constantly in my reality. The wish to let him go free into the monastery of his mind, free of the demands of the body, free of the practical realities of garbage and cars that wouldn't start on cold days, free of baby-sitters and childhood illnesses and money problems and relatives' demands. The wish to let him be—and yet the need to be loved and acknowledged and wanted. He is special; for such men, wives and children are a drain. He needs to be allowed to go alone into the realm of the mind—here is this remarkable capacity for his work, for new frontiers of thinking—leave him be, for God's sake!

The beginning of my work . . .

Ah, there's the place to let go; work—that's the hardest and best place I can go—it will use me up, it will drain me, put out the fire, help me to learn to accept that there will be short periods every once in a while when the hunger and the passion will flare up again, but most of the time I must try to accept—even exult in—this special quality of mind; it is his greatest need and offers his greatest fulfillment—it has been all for many men, and perhaps this isolation of the soul is necessary for greatness. Let me be proud to partner it, let that be enough. And so the demands, the screaming, grow less for sex—but always more for other things; support and help in Julie's problems of life—more and more leaning on *his* growing understanding and deepening love for her, and always still, I talk and talk and talk of *my* feelings and *my* growing and *my* experiencing of myself—and always thinking this was communication.

The beginning of understanding of mother love . . .

Slowly but surely, the focus of love shifts; suddenly there is this lovely young woman, warm and tender and giving, and with a light of inner beauty. Who *is* this creature of love? Where could she have come from? How did she know so much about loving? The exultation—somehow she *knew!* Somewhere, she had felt—beneath the screaming, guilty, anxious, self-hating mother, the wanting, the crying—the wishing to love freely and whole. And underneath the impatient, distracted, often disappearing father, the man who could love, who saw her wonder, who sensed the delight of her. There it was, for us; the wonder of this loving child, and our work—the absorption of it, the giving to it, and the companionship of sharing it.

And then the growing apart when Julie left; what did I think it meant? Less and less need of me, less and less need of bodily feelings and communicating; a turning more and more to things of the mind, each of us alone in our work, for days on end, coming together to talk of work, fewer and fewer loving times, a feeling that I was demanding far more of our being together than he wanted. Dinners alone, night after night, weeks alone in the country, evenings alone, week after week, a division of all labors—less and less reason for coming together, the moments fewer than ever before—and no facing of it—no real looking at it—the very first time in all our years when I seemed to accept, to resign myself—this is the way it is and will be. Friendship, understanding, a moment of glow here and there, and work, almost all of it work. No wondering, really, about what he was thinking or feeling. Just a sense that I was being put at the necessary distance for whatever was going on. Moments of terror—thoughts—could there be someone else? No—impossible! This is the cerebralized man—it's his work, his absorption with ideas—and, I guess, being married to me too long; the waning years, the loss of interest—another stage in the long pattern of feeling my unattractiveness.

The happy moments that comfort, for a while; the occasional shared pleasure in the seashore, the long bike rides, the lying in the sun, listening to the surf. And then, suddenly, the sharp pain, the sudden faintness—where is he? Is he with someone else? The time there was no answer at home, even at two or three A.M. when I was traveling; the return of panic—and the quick denial of it.

The trip to Europe—the disappointment and the fatigue and the lack of any of the usual exhilaration that always before had come with traveling and being alone together; the blaming it on the weather, and tiredness. The confusions and the losing things—a feeling once or twice that now we could not even travel together—that this one source of never-ending closeness was deserting us, and that he really wanted to travel alone, without the encumbrances of my needs—for a room with a bath, for comfort. . . .

The time of beginning to know . . .
The envelope—the name—the letter grabbed with strange speed, the limbo feeling as we got on the plane—it cannot be. There is too much trust, too much friendship—too much love—even that—still, yes, it could not happen. And not knowing—and the lies—it is out of the question.

Let there be oblivion for what has been . . .
The confrontation—all night, all day, the weeping, the shock, the feeling that it is impossible that I am going on living—how can one go on living—how can one go on feeling and breathing when one has died? Who, after all, is this man?
Evil. Cruel beyond understanding; able to take the chance of hurting me more terribly than anyone has ever hurt me before. His mother in him—cold, unloving, and deceitful—a liar and a cheat—everything a lie, nothing good, ever. Sheer, unmitigated cruelty on a level never imagined. Mostly the deception—how could it have gone on for so long? Didn't it matter? Didn't the corruption of all trust matter at all? Everything a lie—the loving and giving, the enthusiasm for my life and growing, the encouragement, the support, the tenderness, the taking care of me—all nothing, all never existing. The end wiping out every beginning.
How did it happen? What must I look at? *His* fault, *his* weakness, *his* meanness of spirit, *his* hostility, *his* hatred. *He* is a bad human being, an evil man. And then *his shock*, a momentary awareness of his pain—his holding me, his trying

to say it was never very much—my grabbing at the still lying thread of hope—it wasn't anything, just needed reassurance of sex, even the hope it might help us—no, I can't believe that. There is the loneliness of his silences—no confessions, no exposure, no explainings, no sharing of that part of his life—only somewhere, for me to try to touch, some awareness that he is still here for me, he has not left; *he has not said anything about leaving*; what can that mean?

He says he has been fragmented—many men, living separately in his body—he says yes, the lying must have finally become intolerable—or why else did he read the letter where I could see it? I try to see it as his torture and none of my own; just another and new expression of his failure, his ruptured soul, his never-healed wounds of childhood—yes, that's it, he's a cripple, and I am good and strong.

But when he tries desperately to say the things that he has never been able to say, while I talked our way through married life, I try to begin to understand. He says that there is "too much history" for us to overcome, and I try to figure out what he means. Is it that there are so many things about me he dislikes? I see in his eyes he wishes he could reassure me, but that he wants to be honest, at last. AT LAST. I think he is trying to learn to talk to me—and I begin to wonder how I could have managed to talk so well for so long, that I never noticed he could not talk to me about what really mattered most. I want to tell him never to touch me again, and what I feel is that I never needed more for him to touch me. Work goes on; there are times alone for me.

I want to leave him; I want to try to make him suffer some part of what I'm suffering; and the worst of it is, I am not at all sure that my leaving would do that; nothing he has ever said to me has made me feel he needed me as much as I needed him; I cannot imagine his ever saying he needed

me *more* than I needed him. That seems quite impossible
—and therefore terrible. I feel the need of love as I have
never felt it before, and I want to kill him, torture him—
but be held close. Every hour of every day, she is in front
of my eyes—dressed, undressed, holding his hand, touching
his body, kissing his lips—somehow always quiet—and I guess
that's because he has told me, with a bright triumph in his
eyes, that she never made any conditions, never asked any
questions, accepts what she can have. I know that I am being
attacked, but I am not ready to face it. What does he really
mean about this quiet acceptance, without claims? He talks
about how it might have been, for us, if we had gone to
bed together when we first met; his feeling that for us it
was right to move quickly into passion, to risk all, let it be
all—and I begin to remember at what arm's length I held
him—not just then, but even after we were engaged; I could
not let go; I was a child of my generation and my home—
but he is right; there was something so unusual about our
first awakening to each other, and I begin to regret that I
was so much a middle-class infant, so scared of life, rather
than a passionate and giving woman (like Julie!) who could
have said "Yes!" to life, then.

I begin to see the dimensions of the man. The suffering,
the absolute refusal to settle for less than being all, the
inability to say what he was feeling, and the degree to which
he had always been quite overwhelmed by the person I
seemed to him to be, his fear of hurting me, his constant
quest to make me happy, but trying to do it by enduring
his own quiet despair. The anger there, always, in the impotence; the feeling of being imprisoned by the conditions
of marriage; the despair at too high a price for loving, *of
being owned by me.*

Passion and sensuality rush back, flood me with cravings,

consume me with feelings that have been repressed all of my life—the terrible cry for him, the need, the opening to my need—and then the sudden knowledge; *there are no conditions.* The wave of lust and loving cannot be denied— whatever it can be, I want, with no conditions. Divorce, if he wants it—but will he let me have an affair with him? On any terms he wants to make . . .

And then the miracle of myself unfolding, of giving up and giving in, of being the receiver, the receptor, the wonder of it, lying there, opened up to life, opened up with a vulnerability I have never had the courage to allow before, the completion of myself in becoming the vessel of *his* needs; the wonder and the exultation in a kind of sensuality I have never experienced before—sex with tears, sex with the shaking off of all the shoulds—there, in utter nakedness of soul, sex with holding nothing back—the passivity of wanting nothing but to be there with him.

The heights of unknown ecstasy, followed by the black pit of despair, as I keep moving back into *my* needs, *my* feelings—always back to *my* hurt—back and forth between giving and demanding—until, until. . . .

The surcease from pain and the wonder at this man . . .
We are surprised to discover that we both now wish we could have another child! A rebirth for us. We are embarrassed and overcome with strange feelings. I see something in his face, a gleam of pleasure at the fantasy that such a thing might happen between us. Craziness! I go into the worst depression of all, where weeping will not stop, even when people are around; I want to be loved but I cannot go near Jerry or ask for comfort this time. We seem to have come to an end, a bottom; I see no way up. And then it

seems to have something to do with that feeling about a baby. We begin, faltering, to try to talk about it again. He tells me he was afraid of hurting Julie—as he'd been hurt—and this kept him from a fuller pleasure in fatherhood. We weep for what might have been; there is a wrenching and a tearing inside me; I cry most of all for Julie—for the limitations in pleasure for both of us, in our emotional cripplings; the burden on a baby—how terrible and cruel—I want another chance—I want to hold her again, my baby, I want to love her for being a baby, to love her without wanting her to give me what Jerry could not give.

We are rocked. And close—and yet the visions of Nina and Jerry together come back again. I wonder—will I suffer with it forever, even when so much good is happening for us? And then—he says two things that seem to change everything, although I know they happen only because I have been getting ready and can understand them.

First he says, sleepily, one morning, "Do you love me?" It is so easy to answer, and I think little about it, until he leaves, and then suddenly I am in shock; never, since the day we met, has he ever asked me that; I have told him all the time—but somehow I know that *his asking* is a turning point in our lives, and that everything is different because he asked me. I am flooded with compassion and tenderness. He can be vulnerable now, know his feelings—because I am no longer choking him with my needs.

And then, when I say that I am beginning to understand that he is a man who hungers for life and could not ever give up, he says, very simply and quietly, "If I gave up, I knew I would die." There it is at last. The man he is. The passion for life, the hunger to fight his devils and come alive, the unbelievable struggle not merely to survive but to conquer. Don Quixote. Zorba. A wild and passionate man, dancing in the sun on a Greek shore, the exulting cry in his throat, that he is alive and can feel and knows he is a man. A MONK? My God, what a case of mistaken identity—which we both share equally—his flaw in not being able to ever tell me, my flaw in never listening to the ways in which he tried to tell me, without language.

There he is—exulting in his manhood, stretching his soul to the sun, shouting to the gods that he is come alive and whole, at last—and knows what it is he searches for—only everything, only all there can ever be—only being alive in every cell, only acknowledging a passion for life that cannot be denied another moment.

The Unknown Man? If that were so I would be shocked and frightened by this wildly alive creature. And yet he seems utterly familiar to me—always known. Ah, yes, of course; this man is the boy I met all those years ago, a boy who wrote me passionately sensual letters, who wanted to make love to me the first night we met; the man who wanted us both to throw away all the shoulds, all the rules, all the conventions of life, and fly into life, with no reservations, no demands, no claims, except just BEING. This adventurer. This man of heroic proportions. This glorious man. Always known—and finally discovered. I am at peace.

⌒ SEVEN MONTHS

Eve has been suggesting for quite a while that maybe I ought to go somewhere by myself for a few days. I just haven't been able to force myself to do it, until this past weekend. It was quite an experience.

I decided to go to a motel on a very isolated cove on the ocean which Jerry and I had discovered by accident about five years ago. For some reason it was an area that had remained unspoiled—very natural and not touristy at all. I remembered that there was a long sandbar, covered with tall dune grass, and if you watched the tides carefully you could walk for miles in absolute solitude, far beyond the few private houses in the area. I had no idea what it would be like now —and realized it might have become a development of three thousand houses or a shopping center—but, happily, it was unchanged.

Eve feels that one of my most pressing problems is my fear of being alone, my dependence on Jerry. Whenever there have been separations other than those due to work schedules, they have always been initiated by Jerry, never by me.

I felt nervous and depressed when I rented the car and began the two-hour drive. But it was early morning, the traffic wasn't bad at all, and I began to feel a sense of exhilaration. I was proud of myself that I didn't get lost—it was a tricky place to find after all these years, along remote, rural roads toward the end of the trip. I was delighted that it was still an underdeveloped area even after all this time. The woman who runs the motel said she remembered me, and whether she did or not, she was very nice and made me feel welcome.

I felt tired with the effort of making the trip alone, sat outside in the sun reading, walked to a little grocery store for some supplies, explored along the beach for just a few minutes, and then went indoors, made myself some soup and a hamburger, watched television. I went to bed early.

thinking I was tired enough to sleep, but kept tossing and turning and finally took a tranquilizer.

When I woke up, the sun was shining—it was a gorgeous, warm day. And, best of all, the tide was really out, so I could walk along the sandbar. I had some coffee and cookies, took some bread for the sea gulls, and started walking. Going past the houses I remembered having looked at with Jerry, I felt a wave of terrible sadness. They were old houses, built at least a hundred years before, and Jerry and I had agreed that was the perfect way to live—looking out at the sea, across beautiful, old lawns. I thought to myself: The last time we were here, I was an Innocent—a kind of psychological virgin; nothing could ever come between Jerry and me. We had problems, and sometimes they upset me very much, but we belonged to each other.

As I walked along now, I had a sense that the bond was broken, that I felt like half of one whole person—it was as if one person had been split down the middle and that I was trying to walk along with one arm and one leg. But that was such an ugly image. I sat down on a rock and looked out at the water. Maybe this physical image was just as ugly as if one thought of it as a psychological image. If I believed that Jerry and I had been one whole person, then of course there would be an ugliness in every respect in being divided in half.

But how does one become a whole person, alone, after having had such a distorted idea for such a long time? By being brave—the way I'd been brave to come here alone, I told myself. But it didn't work. A terrible depression settled over me. I thought of walking to the end of the sandbar— it must have been a mile or two ahead of me—and just staying there until the tide came in, and drowning. Better to die than to be half a human being.

I was scaring the hell out of myself. I decided that maybe physical exercise would help, so I walked fast along the water's edge until I got well past the last house and was walking by the tall grass. After a while, I couldn't see a house or a boat or a person: just me, lost and alone, with sand, water, shells, sandpipers, sea gulls, blue sky, and the sound of the tall grass shushing in a little breeze. I suddenly felt a great sense of exhilaration—and then, to my shock and surprise—very sexually aroused. It was weird! A kind of crazy exultation—and the sense that I had to do something about it. I started to run toward the grass; it was like being another person, on the outside, watching yourself doing something crazy that you knew you'd never do and couldn't be doing now; it had to be someone else.

I lay down in the grass; there was absolutely nothing in sight—I was completely hidden. It crossed my mind that I could probably lie there for years and nobody would ever be able to find me. I had never been so absolutely alone in all my life. I began sobbing—and masturbating—simultaneously. It was some kind of baptism—the most ultimate and final loneliness, and then the reaffirming of being alive, by God, *I* could do that for *myself*! It lasted a long time; it was frenzied and accompanied by sobbing, moaning—and then silence. I lay in the grass, exhausted, depleted, looking up at the sky, touching the grasses and sand under my hands. I was *not* half a person—I was whole. All by myself.

Finally I sat up and looked around me. The waves were much closer, and I realized the tide was coming in. I got up, went to the water, waded, washed; the water was still too cold for swimming. I threw the bread to the sea gulls, and then realized I was starving. I walked quickly back toward the houses, the motel. In some places the water had already gotten quite deep, and I felt scared; suppose I had gone all the way out to the very end—could I have gotten back, in such cold water? It seemed like a narrow escape both figuratively and literally—as if my life could have gone either way. I decided I wanted a seafood meal in a really good restaurant. That would be another first. Ordinarily, if I was alone I'd eat at home or at a counter somewhere. The idea of sitting at a table in a restaurant all alone seemed embarrassing, unbearably lonely. But not now. I wanted LOBSTER! And I wanted someone TO WAIT ON ME! I changed my clothes, took one of the magazines I'd brought along, and drove to a seafood restaurant Jerry and I had discovered last time we were here. At one time it had been a ferryboat, and you could sit on the deck and look out over the water. The restaurant was almost deserted, and I asked for a table facing the water. I ordered New England clam chowder, steamers, and a lobster! I'd thought I'd want to read while I was eating, but I discovered that I didn't mind eating alone at all, and just looked at the water. On a note of triumph I thought to myself, Hell, if you can masturbate in the sand dunes and enjoy it thoroughly, eating alone is an anticlimax!

For a flash, I thought it would be nice to be able to say that to Jerry. He would have laughed, appreciated it. I suddenly missed him terribly. But then the food came, and I ate ravenously.

For the rest of the time, I tried to think very carefully about what I felt like doing. If I chose the right thing, that was fine; if I changed my mind, I did something else. The following day it rained, and I started to drive to the nearest town to see a movie; then, halfway there, I decided I didn't feel like doing that at all, and went back to the motel. The day I was supposed to go home, I thought I'd want to go back to my sandbar—maybe repeat the events of the first day —but by the time I'd reached the beach, I knew that was a great mistake. It occurred to me that I was tired of being alone and had nothing further to prove to myself. I sat on the lawn in front of the motel and began to talk to a couple who had tried to be friendly the day before, but I had cut them off. I liked them—and they liked me! They invited me to have lunch with them—they were going to use the outdoor fireplace to cook some fish they had caught. I had a lovely time!

Driving home was the only bad part of the trip. The traffic was heavy and I got very tired. I couldn't decide whether to stay on the highway or get off. I wondered if Jerry would worry if I got home later than I'd said I'd be home. My new freedom and independence seemed to be crumbling. By the time I got home, I was cranky and un-communicative. Jerry tried to hug me, said he'd missed me. He asked if I'd had a good time. Suddenly I knew I did not want to tell him what had happened. *My first secret!* It oc-curred to me that I didn't love him any less just because a part of my life was private.

⌒ EIGHT MONTHS

We are lying in bed. My head is on Jerry's shoulder. I have been weeping quietly. No demands, no accusations—just a return of terrible sadness. So many months have passed, and yet there are times when the pain is still knife sharp. Jerry came home late tonight. When he called and said he wasn't coming home for supper, I wanted desperately to ask why, but I didn't. I took a long walk, huddled inside an old raincoat, wearing dark glasses in the dark. Were they together?

I walked for miles, came home, sat on the window ledge, looking at the lights, the traffic below. Was it worthwhile to try to go on living? What was the point? Again there are thoughts of suicide. If I jumped, how long would I stay conscious? Maybe if I jumped, I'd still be lying there, a mashed-up heap of blood and bones, when Jerry came home. Maybe he'd be the one to find me!

By the time I hear Jerry's key in the door, I have recognized the return of rage, and it is now subsiding. He finds me weeping quietly and holds me. In spite of everything that has happened, the only place in all the world where I feel safe, comforted, is in his arms. It's crazy!

He says, "Come to bed. I have something to tell you." We lie in silence for a few minutes. I begin to realize something important has happened; we have reached a new crossroads, and Jerry has decided on which road we are taking. I move out of his arms, sit up, blow my nose—wait. Then he sits up, turns on the light. He looks solemn, and I allow myself to see suffering in *his* eyes. He says, "It's all over."

"What's all over?" I ask stupidly. I knew instantly what he meant. But I want it said, to make it real. "The relationship with Nina. It has been coming for a long time. It had to go one way or the other."

I think that what he means is that Nina had settled for what she could have of him for two years, but now wanted much more. What an ironic twist. I started loving with conditions and I gave them up. Nina loved without conditions at first—and maybe developed some later. Of course, that's the reason for the "accident" of my reading the letter. The decision had really been made then.

"Are you sure?" I ask. "Are you very unhappy?"

"It was time," he says. "I'm telling you now because I thought it might make you feel better." For a moment I am touched; he feels he is giving me the ultimate gift. Then I begin to get angry. I feel the most amazing connectedness to Nina. We are both pawns in this man's life! He changes our fate by what he decides to do about us! Nuts to *that*! "Don't do me any favors," I yell. "What's done is done, and this doesn't change anything." But of course it has changed everything. Even while I'm denying it, a wave of relief passes through me. Thank God! He's chosen me. I can't help myself; I love him and need him. So did Nina. At last I can begin to feel compassion for her. Suppose *I* had lost him.

Will the images of them in bed together begin to diminish, fade? Will there ever be a time when I might actually forget —not care? Somehow, right now, neither of us wants to talk any more. We turn out the light, each lying separately, thinking, wanting to be alone. For the first time I begin to have a new set of images: Nina telling Jerry her troubles, leaning on him, letting him know that she was having forever-feelings, needed him. I see them *talking*, and feel shocked that all this time I have been so preoccupied with the physical part. There must have been so much more.

I search for his hand in the dark. "It must hurt a lot," I whisper. "To have hurt two people you love. To leave something behind you—a whole history—" He squeezes my hand back, but he doesn't want to pursue this further. "Yeah," he says, and turns away. I realize that no matter where we go in our marriage, Nina is now part of both of us, forever. We are all three scarred. But I have the possibility of renewal with Jerry. I hope she won't be alone for long; I hope she isn't suffering as much as I would if I had been the one left behind.

~ TEN MONTHS

There are sudden moments when one senses life so deeply. I was just listening to the seven o'clock news on television and heard an announcement that there had been a bomb explosion in a building I was in at exactly this time yesterday. Twenty-four hours—or I might have been one of those dead bodies the police and firemen were tying into bundles. At one point, watching television, I saw a hand dangling out of the canvas bag and a policeman shove it back in. Along with the shock and sadness for whoever that woman may have been, there is also the sharp awareness—suppose it had been ME. We are always so close to death, but in the bustle of daily living this knowledge recedes into unawareness, numbness. It is good to be forced to think about it.

In spite of everything, I WANT TO LIVE! I savor my life; it is sweet and good in so many ways. I will never give it up without a fight; I am sure I will go kicking and screaming into the night. I am greedy for more and more and more of living, curious and full of wonder and hope. Depressed and sad I may get—and I have surely ranted and raved against life and will again, for certain; but when the chips are down, I want every bit of this agonizingly short time of living I can have.

Midway
The Second Year

ᘚ *ONE*

*A*s I weep in her office, Eve asks, "What do you really want?" I suddenly begin to see all the ambiguities of wants:

WANTED: Oblivion: waking from it as a dream; it never happened; there is no one else.
AND YET: Not really that, for all these months of growing toward love would never have happened.

WANTED: There was never anyone else: just this new affair of the heart, between us, all alone.
AND YET: Not that either—for there was a price, a claim, a need that there be no space between us, no privacy, no separateness, and for such a man, that was inviting a death of the soul. I want it, but I cannot have it, for there are new things that I want more. Even privacy for myself.

WANTED: The promise of a perfect future; the utter solitude and peace of being one, in ways never dreamed of before; The heights of passion and tenderness, the secrecy of it, the never-ending hunger for each other.
AND YET: Not that either. Again a condition, a demand, an

insurance policy for the future—which Jerry cannot give, and can be required only of a lesser man.

WANTED: To be a woman—a woman of so great a heart and such an openness that there is no wanting at all—only a need to give and to be, and to cherish any moment as it comes, with no regrets for when it goes.
AND YET: I am far away from being such a woman. Only for a moment, or a day, can I be a seeker after life, a companion to Jerry's inner travels. One step at a time, one step at a time—away from making claims, of demanding instead of inviting.

WANTED: Only the courage to do the growing.

✍ TWO

It is incredible—shocking—how little either Jerry or I have understood how our feelings about ourselves were subtly undermining our relationship with each other. Jerry's fear of displeasing me—without ever consciously facing the dread that he wasn't good enough and I might leave him; my clinging to him, demanding, controlling—in a panic that he might realize I wasn't good enough for him.

One night last week we suddenly had an impulse to look at some old photograph albums—ourselves as children, as adolescents. We were adorable! It is still hard for me to see that in myself, and Jerry in himself, but we are beginning to understand what the other is saying about the objective reality. Jerry had a wistful, sad face, with beautiful, enormous brown eyes. He is wearing a mask—there is a blandness that we can now both see. I was a cute little girl! Where did I get the feeling that I was monstrous? Both of us! And most other children growing up. I've asked other people lately—and maybe out of about fifty people about our age or older, *only one* remembered herself as "a pretty child." And just as I thought, Well, at least one, she added, "But of course that didn't help much because I felt I was awfully dumb!" What is it that *happens* to children that seems to leave so many of us with such a residue of self-contempt?

Eve and I were talking about this, and she said that probably there is a different constellation of factors in each child's life. I tried to think what it could have been in mine. "It must be a sort of childish fantasy—a grim fairy tale!" I said. She appreciated that, and then she said, "So *write* it!"

THE GRIM FAIRY TALE

Once upon a time, there was a teeny-tiny girl who lived in a enchanted castle. Nobody knew she was there. She could play and watch the grown-ups all day long. She lived in a secret place inside herself, and she danced in the noonday sun. Sometimes she turned into a butterfly. Sometimes she flew over the heads of the grown-ups and she saw many things they could not see.

Then one terrible day she turned into a human being. Something happened that made her visible. Where before she felt beautiful, she now felt ugly. Where before she had felt good, she now felt bad. She did not know why. A fairy told her she would have to make a choice. She could go back to being enchanted, but if she did, she would not be able to talk to other people, and they would not be able to see her. Or she could stay human and grow up like other people, and everyone would see her and talk to her and know who she was. The girl decided very quickly; it was too lonely being enchanted. She wanted to be noticed—and loved. In one moment she made the decision, and for all the rest of her life she was able to live with other people and love them and be loved back, but deep down inside of her there was always a small, sad memory of the time when she had been enchanted and was so beautiful and could float in the air.

A long time passed. She grew up and did many interesting things. She was happy sometimes and sad sometimes. She never forgot the enchanted castle; she had many dreams about it. The time came when she began to wonder if she had made the wrong choice. Being seen and being loved were important—but was it truly worth it, if you always felt ugly and bad? She began to wonder if it really had to be that way—one thing or the other. Perhaps this was an enchantment that she might break, if she could find the secret, the magic formula. There must be a key to this secret someplace deep inside of her. First she would have to find a grown-up woman who was very wise, some special person she had been waiting for all her life; this woman would know what she must do.

One day when she was looking in the mirror, she met this lady, who was beautiful and wise, and the lady gave her some very mysterious tasks to do. First she said, "Find a garden," and the girl found a garden Then she said, "Find someone young to love," and the girl realized that somewhere along the way she had had a daughter, and she began to love her fiercely and proudly, as she never had before. Then the lovely lady said, "It is time you became a writer." And after a while she said, "Now come and look at me in the mirror again," and suddenly the enchanted little girl disappeared. "Here I am, little girl," the lady in the mirror said. "Now you are yourself, and when you walk away from the mirror, you will be seen—and loved—and beautiful."

As I came to the end of my story, having had no idea what I would write or how it would end, I began to weep, but not in pain—more in relief. It was as if some profound change had occurred—some new level of growth had taken place. At first I could only sense this—I had no idea what the story meant. I showed it to Jerry the minute he came home from work and asked him, "Why did this story make me cry with *relief?*"

By the time he'd finished reading it, he was crying, too. "Hey, grown-up lady," he said. "Come *here!*" We held each other tight. I felt some kind of exultation—a sense of accomplishment without the vaguest idea what that accomplishment might be. Jerry was very excited. We sat down to talk about it. He laughed indulgently, as if I were a little girl and Daddy would now explain a few facts of life; I loved it!

"This is the loveliest way I've ever seen it put," he said. "You have written about what it means to become human. You've said it more simply than the psychiatric treatises. One gives up the innocence of babyhood to join the world, and in that process each of us discovers our flaws, our imperfections. We are told what is wrong with us; adults begin correcting us. We get a distorted view of ourselves as being no damned good because people seem to be saying we could be so much better—but nobody can ever be as good as we think we ought to be. I think you have explained why, to some degree, self-hate becomes the enemy we all struggle the hardest to overcome as adults. And we have to do it because the alternative is to refuse to, join in the human condition."

I feel so happy, so relieved. The more I have struggled to discover my own nature, the closer I have come to integration; it is neither grim nor a fairy tale, but a True Love Story—about falling in love with myself. I tell Jerry, "I almost started to say, 'And now I'll live happily ever after,' but in the back of my head I hear a voice telling me that nobody ever remembers this necessary kind of self-loving all the time; you just have to keep trying to remember."

ᘯ THREE

I had a startling experience with Rachel, who I hadn't seen for more than a year. I spent a day visiting her and was surprised to find her looking absolutely sensational, when she's been divorced for just three months. I suppose I expected her to feel even worse than I felt when I first found out about Jerry's affair; after all, in her case, Al wasn't just having an affair—he wanted a divorce.

We made small talk for several hours; I certainly wasn't going to urge her to talk about it if she didn't want to. But she got to it after a while—and her attitude really knocked me out. She was so reasonable, so understanding. Al's relationship with a much younger woman had come on very suddenly, and he came to Rachel, asking for a divorce, almost immediately thereafter. Rachel had been kind, compassionate, accepting.

I knew this had been a satisfying marriage and that Al and Rachel had loved each other; how could she be so calm? I could think of little else for several days; it was a puzzle that I felt I had to put together in order to learn something about myself and Jerry.

It finally dawned on me; it seemed more than likely that unconsciously Rachel had been waiting for this to happen—and she wasn't really very sorry! She had assured me there was no other man yet, and I believe her—but she sure as hell is *ready*! She has had a fascinating job for the past ten years; she's made more money than Al; she's met a great many interesting, successful people and she's traveled a great deal. She would probably never have initiated a divorce—she's a nice, proper lady with traditional notions about marriage and impeccably good manners!—and her work was so engrossing that her marriage just wasn't that important any more. Al was not so crazy; the most poignant part of the story was his comment that he knew she would be reasonable. Rachel felt that was a compliment; I think it was a report on the state of their marriage!

But why my preoccupation? I remember my screaming and raving and wanting to die; my rage. And yet Jerry hadn't even wanted to leave me. Suddenly it all comes clear. Despite the agony we were living through, we were always crazy about each other! I adored Jerry—always felt he was the most fascinating man who ever lived, and I know now that he felt the same way about me. Our struggle with each other and ourselves was *because we had so much to lose*. I wonder if Rachel will ever care that much about someone?

ᨒ *FOUR*

I suddenly realized today how much less often I tell Jerry what I am thinking or feeling. It came as a great shock. I was telling Eve that Jerry and I seem to be going our separate ways a great deal of the time lately. I said, "Jerry seems to be running away from me." Eve asked, "Is he running away from you or running toward his work?" God, what makes that woman so damned perceptive! That's exactly what he's doing. I suppose we have spent so much of our time and energy on The Crisis, that now each of us needs time alone, time to work, time for privacy.

My moods have been very up and down; I've had a lot on my mind. Important, personal thoughts. I told Eve that, much to my surprise, I hadn't been telling Jerry anything about what I was going through. Was I getting more like him? Eve declared that an irrelevant question. "It doesn't matter whether you are becoming more or less like Jerry; the real issue is, are you becoming more like *yourself*?"

ᨒ *FIVE*

Do I dare to allow myself even to have the thought that maybe, after many years of marriage, other lovers can be a source of new ideas and refreshment? It makes me mad that I have such thoughts. It makes me face the fact that I'm changing—and one of the things I'm learning is that it is very painful to give up feelings and attitudes you have had all your life. They may be neurotic or narrow or even anti-life, but they are *one's own,* familiar and comfortable, and I cling to mine. As I change, inexorably, part of me feels it is against my will. And yet there are other times when I feel proud and new, when I realize that I have said something more wise and human than maybe I've ever said before. It happens in conversations with friends and relatives who have all my old assumptions; I find myself arguing from a new position. It shocks me—but then later I have a feeling of lightness and freedom. Margo says she still believes in total fidelity in marriage, and I hear myself saying, "But we live so long now—does it really make sense to make that such an important part of marriage?" Or Suzy gets very uptight about the fact that her daughter has had four affairs (that she knows about) and doesn't seem at all inclined to get married; she calls her promiscuous. "That's ridiculous!" I shout indignantly. "She's a lovely young woman, and you know that each of these relationships have been loving and responsible; you know you've been crazy about her choices. What's the rush? Our children will understand loving in a new open, unselfconscious, giving way that escaped us completely. I think it's great." Who is this talking? I often feel as though I am inside the body of a total stranger.

Sometimes I feel that I have changed as much as I can; I want to scream, "Stop here—I want to get off!" The other day Jerry and I decided to go to see a porno movie; I have already repressed the name of it! They *bore* me so. Am I repressing some deep attraction to them? That seems impossible. If watching other people in the act of sex turned me on, I wouldn't feel unhappy about it—why should I? We could always rush home and pick up where the film left off! But what happens is that if I'm not yawning, I'm laughing. It's nothing but *contortions*. Ridiculous postures that are in no way improved by visualization. Human beings are really put together in a rather ridiculous way, and it seems to me that privacy is really the only antidote to that frailty. It leaves more to the imagination, and touching seems to me to be so much more satisfactory anyway. I suppose it is because it is all so technical. If I could watch Rhett Butler and Scarlett or Heathcliff and Cathy or Romeo and Juliet, I suspect I might be very much aroused. The setting would include the passion of loving, and that I would find exciting. Gyrations amuse me, and then, after a while, I begin to wonder if sex is really as great as I dimly remember it to be. We left after about twenty minutes. Jerry says he feels the same way, but I'm not sure. Maybe without me, he would enjoy it.

When I mentioned it to Eve, we got into a discussion of new ways in sex and the old problem of what is "natural" or "instinctive" and what is learned in behavior and preferences. One can't prove anything either way, but I *feel* as if public sex isn't natural. Eve says it is conditioning at very deep levels, and that I don't have to do anything I don't want to do. I suppose these thoughts derive from a discussion with Jean when she told me that she and Mike have sometimes slept with another woman. They have a number of single women friends, and from time to time three of them have gotten into bed together, nude, and fondled and touched and played—she and the other woman as well as Mike and both women. She has never actually watched while the other two had intercourse—she turns over and goes to sleep or goes into another room—or the other woman leaves if that seems most appropriate. As she describes it, I can understand intellectually that it could be natural and tender.

That's because I love Jean and know that no matter what she did she could not help but do it with integrity and great caring. But I am still shocked and uneasy.

The question is, do I have to change *everything* about myself in order to go on growing as a person? Change for its own sake seems an empty goal. I suppose the issue really is, do I *want* to change—and I have the right to choose among all the possibilities. I realize how many of the things I resist and dislike please other people very much, and some part of me wonders if I lose out. Oral sex for example, which I try to enjoy, but don't. The taboos are so deep and I suspect might only be broken through alcohol or drugs—maybe hypnotism! But is it worth it?

Obviously, if I'm thinking about it so much, I haven't decided if I want to explore new avenues or not. If I were deeply frustrated—or if Jerry seemed deprived—that would make a difference. But we are so *comfortable* with our old ways, and there are moments during orgasm when it seems to me that such excruciating pleasure has gone as far as it can go; any more and I will explode into fragments, to land on the moon in some future age! Do I need an egg in my beer?

༄ SIX

Jerry assures me that the end of the relationship with Nina was not for my sake. He says, "If I had allowed that to be the reason, it would have meant the end of you and me." That seems so cruel and self-centered. And yet, I know what he means: that neither of us must try to own the other's life.

I certainly don't feel any sense of triumph—or even great joy. Just a quiet wonder and a genuine wish that this was right for Jerry. I wish Nina well—she lost the human being I love most in the world. I feel a sense of awe that *I* am loved and that Jerry seems to assume it's an always love. I feel guilty for not wanting to share him, but I accept my jealousy as part of who I am. But I know in some profound way that I am changed, and if such a thing were ever to happen again, I would behave somewhat differently at least. At least I know I can live with it and that I can survive it. I have already done that.

I feel very solemn. Now, with relief, I can see what this affair has done *for* our marriage, for our growing. I am ashamed to even admit it to myself, but now that it's over, I know it was one of the most profound and meaningful events in all our years of marriage. It will remain as a reminder—a warning—that we must respect each other's lives and leave breathing spaces between us—and to say whatever needs saying—I hope so much that at least we've learned that.

The whole thing still seems very strange, unreal. To live so intimately with another human being—and to know nothing of one whole, important part of his life! Jerry tells me nothing of how it broke up—who wanted out, whether Nina is suffering, or already has someone else, what it was they really meant to each other, whether or not they still see each other. I keep hoping someday he'll be able to talk to me about it—but I am sure it will never happen. I think this is partly Jerry's nature—life-style—and partly a loyalty to Nina.

Jerry seems concerned that my relief will make me comfortable and smug. He repeated several times that this must not mean we stop changing and growing. How little he understands what all of this has meant to me! He seems so anxious and insistent, that I find myself wondering if he didn't prolong the relationship or delay telling me about its being over because it was some sort of "weapon" to hold over my head, to force me to examine myself and my life. What a cruel thing that would be—and so lacking in awareness that the processes that have started in me no longer have any direct relationship with his affair.

We are a long way from "arriving" at some new and better way of living together. The wounds and scars are there, permanently. I have no doubt there will be new crises. I dread that knowledge—hate it—and am also curious! Is it just vindictivenes or something more that now makes me wonder if *I* might ever be the wanderer? The thought scares me but also intrigues me—but also horrifies me. I suppose at the very least it would help me to understand all that has happened.

If it ever happens to Jerry again, will I behave differently? I don't know. I'm not sure. It would bother me terribly, but I think I would be less obsessed and threatened. I have a greater sense of my own worth; for one thing, I am a survivor! I survived! That gives me a sense of pride and self-confidence. For another, my subtle claim on Jerry, that he was responsible for making me feel secure and happy, is gone. I know I can live and work—and love!—in the midst of anguish.

It would be good for me to have an affair. Then the mystery part of it would be over; I'd understand the parts I don't understand now. But I'd have to be in love, and that means falling out of love with Jerry—so it could never be the same thing.

I spent the weekend in the country with Evelyn, who is so caught between her two loves. Richard now knows; Evelyn is trying to give up Carl. My own wound opened again in watching and listening to her pain. So much of what she says about Richard applies to me. At one point she said, "Richard is so preoccupied with his own pain that he can't see or tolerate mine." That was just the way I behaved with Jerry. Richard also feels abandoned, afraid of rejection, unable to imagine the possibility of Evelyn's loving two men. He sounds so much like me—and then I see how the partner is suffering. I couldn't when it was Jerry, but now it is my best friend, and I understand Jerry's pain by watching hers. Richard does just what I did—expresses his rage and his pain in such a way that she feels it is all her burden. After his explosions, he feels better; she is left shaking and shattered. What she is really doing is serving as an interpreter between Jerry and myself.

Jerry called and Evelyn overheard my half of the conversation. Afterward she said, "I know you don't mean to do it, but you asked about twenty questions about where Jerry was going, what he'd been doing, whom he'd been seeing. It must drive him crazy, just as it does me. It doesn't really mean anything—I really prefer being truthful—and often what I'm doing is completely insignificant, but I get *wild* when Richard asks me what I'm going to be doing all day when he leaves in the morning. Jerry and I need freedom and privacy, and that doesn't mean we are necessarily going to do anything wrong!"

I was just trying to make conversation on the phone. The truth is, I no longer care as much or am as interested as I once must have been in Jerry's every move. I suppose it's just an old habit. I'll have to watch myself more closely. Evelyn can teach me about Jerry; they are so much alike. Interesting—my best love and my best friend—both needing to be free. And I chose both of them!

～ *SEVEN*

Jerry has been my Rock of Gibraltar since my mother died. He helps me to allow whatever feelings I need to have to come to the surface; he helps me not to be afraid of the pain, which comes in waves that seem unbearable, but which I know I must experience. At first I thought the pain was the same as the way I felt when I found out about Nina. But it isn't like that at all, because then I felt alone, bereft—cut off from Jerry—and now he is there for me in every way. In the midst of my own grief, I see something wonderful; he is so much more in touch with his own feelings. There was a time when he would have been stoic, silent, unmoved; then, about six months later, he would discover that he had been grieving. Now the feelings come almost as quickly as my own. He lets his sense of loss show, too.

We cling to each other. He understands that even though I am almost a half century old, I am still a broken child. He reassures me that acceptance will come, but he warns me that there will always be piercing moments of pain; they will just come less and less frequently as time passes. Somehow that makes the present anguish more endurable. I can't believe that I will never touch my mother again. I smell her perfume, I touch the things she has touched; how can *things* survive, when it is the *person* who is real?

I am flooded by memories—both good and bad. I am a motherless child; it seems incredible—something one is never prepared for; it changes everything, forever. I remember

how mad she made me, sometimes, how she made me laugh—
our special kinds of jokes. I remember her fears, her rigidi-
ties—and then I remember that she loved me more, in a
special and different way, than anyone else in the world.

Jerry helps me to remember it all—not to try to shut out
the times I hated my mother. It's all of a piece, he tells me;
keep the humanity in; don't try to shut out one part, because
if you do, you lose everything.

I find myself regretting terribly that my mother knew
about what was happening to Jerry and me. It was childish
to give in weakly to my need for sympathy. My shock and
pain about Nina were, in a way, the worst of what I got
from my mother; her rules—a certain puritanical, childishly
overromanticized view of life. But I'm glad I fought that
part of her in me, and somehow, feeling that I am succeed-
ing, makes me feel freer to remember the good parts.

I have been leaning on Jerry so much these past few weeks.
I can hardly bear to be away from him—I need so much
holding and comforting. This morning I told him that all
this dependency is frightening me. It made him feel imprisoned for so many years. Jerry tells me that *needing* and
owning are totally different things, that I have changed far
more than I realize.

Suddenly I know it is true. In my mourning, I need his
love and support and closeness, but I don't assume it as a
right—an obligation on his part—it is a miracle, a gift he
gives me.

There is no way of anticipating how one will feel about
the death of a parent. There are days when I can't stop
crying for hours on end. Or I will seem to have cried myself out, and then I'll see a woman on the street or on a bus
with my mother's posture, or a coat like hers, and a sense of
desolation and loss overwhelms me again. I carry a pair of

sunglasses with me everywhere, for I never know when the crying will start again.

And because this is a kind of behavior that has only happened once before, I find myself remembering when I found out about Nina. I realize now that much of my behavior was mourning, not anger. I was mourning for illusions that had to be given up, mourning for parts of myself that I would have to let go. It is a constant source of amazement to me how hard it is to give up neurotic parts of oneself, even when they get in the way, impede growth, make one unhappy. But they are so deep and so familiar. All that weeping and screaming was, at least in part, my unconscious awareness that that crisis in my marriage meant there were foolish little-girl things about me that had to go, that I would have to examine myself and live and love in new ways.

And of course I was right. Looking back, I know there are parts of who-I-was that simply don't exist any more. It was right and necessary to mourn as I did. You need good-byes even for things you must get rid of.

I had a dream last night that disturbed me very much. It was one of the most unusual I have ever had. It was a whole story—as if I'd written a piece of fiction for a magazine. I was so glad I had an appointment with Eve today! In the dream I was walking along a street in the theater section of the city. It was a lovely, brisk, sunny fall day, and I was feeling wonderful. Suddenly I passed a small French restaurant that seemed very familiar in some strange way. I felt drawn inexorably to the black iron gate out in front. I stopped, went down a couple of steps, and looked through the gate. On the left was a tiny little garden with a fountain in the middle, flagstones, a bench, lovely bushes, flowering plants. On the right was a door leading to a restaurant, now dark and deserted.

I tried to force myself to leave and go on down the street, but I couldn't. I had to get inside that garden. I opened the gate and walked inside. Suddenly I was a little girl, sitting on the bench, holding a rag doll. I felt perfectly happy, utterly at peace. I listened to the splash of the fountain and threw pebbles into the basin. Then I smelled fresh bread baking, and I stole into the dining room just long enough to take some bread and run back out into the garden.

Suddenly a furious man came to the door of the restaurant. He began screaming at me. He wore a large white apron and a chef's hat. He looked very menacing, and I was terrified. He threatened to call the police, told me to get out of the garden, screamed at me for stealing his bread. I wanted to get up and run, but I just could not move. I woke up feeling that I was in great danger, but that I had to stay in the garden.

When I told Eve the dream, she asked me to talk back to the chef, now that I was awake. As my grown-up self, I should explain why that little girl was in the garden, make him understand why she needed to be there.

"I can't do it," I said. Eve wanted to know why not. "I just can't." "You mean you can't speak for yourself? Come to the defense of that poor little girl?" Eve asked. "I guess not," I said, getting very mad at Eve for not leaving me alone.

But she was not to be denied. "Well, if you can't help yourself, is there anyone who could help you?" she wanted to know. That was better. "Yes, that's easy," I said. "You could help me." "All right, then, pretend you are me and talk to that chef," she ordered. As Eve, I said:

"Listen here, mister—stop yelling at that poor little girl. She's doing nothing to hurt your restaurant or your garden. You should be ashamed of yourself for scaring a child that way. All she needs is a little nourishment. She needs a place to be quiet and alone, and to eat some of your delicious bread. Is that so terrible?"

Eve was grinning. "That wasn't so bad, was it?" I was astonished. That little girl was me; why couldn't I have protected her, instead of needing Eve to do it? "Well," Eve said, "it may have seemed to you that you were relying on me—but, after all, you are the person who spoke for me!"

I felt tricked and also exultant. It's true. The dream and the words have been mine. And they have been a demand that I pay attention to the child inside myself, who must be nourished if I am to feel alive, if I am to go on growing.

"I get the message," I said dryly. "I guess that's the answer to the question I raised last week about whether or not Jerry and I could afford to buy that bungalow in the woods. I see we have to."

EIGHT

I had dinner with Margaret last night. She's a remarkable woman who has had a fascinating life, and I have become very fond of her. I really enjoy listening to her stories. One of the ones I love best is how, before she left Germany, she scolded two young Nazi officials when they were tormenting an old Jew and told them they should have been spanked more often; she just got mad. They were too surprised to do anything. I have enormous admiration for her courage and for how cheerfully she puts up with difficulties. We are opposites in so many ways, since I rave and rant at the slightest provocation, and she laughs at life's inequities.

Last night we talked for the first time about our first impressions of each other. She didn't like me either at that first meeting in the theater. I suppose we were both defensive; the relationship between a wife and her husband's psychotherapist is not unlike daughter and mother-in-law, I guess. I told Margaret how uneasy I had been when she first indicated that she wanted to meet me, that we could have a social relationship with each other as she already had with Jerry, as well as being his therapist. Margaret operates on the same revolutionary premise as Eve that grown-up people can have a variety of relationships with each other and that one does not have to interfere with the other! They both seem to think that Jerry and I are special, and don't want us to be just patients, but friends as well. Jerry and I both find this works out very well. We all shift roles quickly and appropriately. Jerry takes Margaret to the doctor sometimes, since it's hard for her to travel alone; it was Jerry and I that helped Eve recognize she was somatizing some tensions and it was time for her to go back into therapy! We can start a session by discussing mutual friends, or Eve's latest insights into herself—but if I feel the need for immediate attention, with some urgent anguish or confusion—or even an exultancy—she's all there for me, alert, professional, that special kind of listening that brings focus and insight in its wake.

But back to Margaret. I told her last night how embarrassed I had felt about meeting her, how I even hated her for not telling Jerry he just couldn't have an affair! She laughs at me—the kind of laugh that seems a genuine merriment, as if she really enjoys what a silly, naive little girl I was (and still cling to being even now sometimes). She's genuinely curious to know where I got such ideas, such as thinking that she would condemn me because my husband needed to have an affair. Apparently her parents were the exact opposite of mine—free-thinkers, uninhibited about sex, long before such attitudes were open. They were closet hippies in the 1920s!

As I listened to her laugh and see the wisdom and charm and courage of this marvelous woman, I think to myself that she isn't only a therapeutic influence in Jerry's life. The fact that she sought me out, that she enjoys my friendship—that she obviously has great affection for me—has been another part of the healing and the growing that I have been experiencing. I would expect my own therapist to care for me— that is essential to the relationship; to have a similarly warm relationship with one's spouse's therapist is, I think, something that adds to one's own growing geometric progression. Of course, Eve feels exactly the same way about Jerry. I suppose what happens is that more and more we realize that we are both lovable people, that our problems are not now, and have never been, those of adversaries, but of two crippled people trying desperately to become more alive and ourselves. It is terribly important to my growth that Eve can be so alert to Jerry's needs and vulnerabilities and can help to sensitize me; and I'm sure the same thing happens between Margaret and Jerry.

At any rate, when I came home last night, I felt grateful that Margaret and I hadn't remained strangers, and that I'd been able to talk to her about my discomfort about meeting her. What seems so remarkable, and makes me feel terribly safe—and lucky!—is that Jerry and I could switch therapists at any point, if we wanted to, and know beyond any shadow of doubt that we would be just as lovingly and insightfully guided and encouraged. It seems to me that it is one of the most hopeful and remarkable aspects of our marriage.

✐ *NINE*

A woman I know only slightly called this morning. Once, at a dinner party, I had mentioned the fact that I was in therapy, and she recalled that she'd been intrigued by my description of Eve. She wondered if I'd give her Eve's number. Of course I did, but she seemed to want to talk to me— as if she would explode before she could dial another number! She is considering having an affair! A man she's known since childhood. They were in love but too young, and both sets of parents insisted they separate after high school and go to different colleges. Both had been married to other people—unhappily—for many years. They feel affection and compassion for their respective spouses, and are unable to leave them, but realize they still love each other. She wanted my opinion. It was a pretty hysterical situation! When she described her husband—a rigid, frightened man who could not change, I heard myself encouraging her to live her life! How weird that she was so ready to confide in me. Maybe she's a crazy lady; but it also occurs to me that many people discuss such issues quite candidly now, and that I may be the only throwback to Victorian times extant!

I am trying so terribly hard to be open and giving, without strings, but I *just can't.* I am monogamous to my deepest roots. If I try to imagine turning for comfort to some new man, I immediately visualize a courtship and a falling in love—and a marriage. It's just the way my mind works. I need to be all for one person and have him feel that way about me. I still cannot imagine loving two people at one time. It still disgusts me. And yet I could see good reasons for this woman having an affair. I *am* changing.

ᴄ⁓ᴏ *TEN*

After four years of widowhood, Catherine has a boyfriend! She looked radiant the first time I saw her, after two or three dates. Yesterday, over the phone, she sounded terrible. Apparently she and Sam had tried to have sex relations for the first time. "He couldn't perform," she told me gloomily.

I found myself recoiling from that phrase—and realized once again how much I have learned and changed. We arranged to meet, and I spent about two hours trying to give her the benefit of my life experience! Sam was widowed just four months ago. His wife was ill for many years. From what he has told Catherine, it sounds as if he had a lot of unshed tears, of mourning, to deal with. He's probably in a deep depression he doesn't know anything about consciously. I explained how often depression interferes with sexual activity. I also tried to explain the vicious cycle: anxiety—inability to have an erection—more anxiety—more inability, etc., etc. Catherine seems to have little idea of the terror men feel when they are impotent. It is so different for women, who can pretend. It may be dishonest and destructive, but there is still less feeling of failure. It may be upsetting not to have an orgasm, but a woman can still participate, and that makes all the difference in the world in attitudes and reactions. Men are so terribly threatened—

especially older men who were taught all their lives that the burden of sexuality rested with them.

I told Catherine that love and passion could be expressed in a variety of other ways than just in the sex act itself; that when impotence occurs, it is a fine opportunity to explore other aspects of one's sensuality—of giving and receiving pleasure. The way she listened, I found myself wondering about how little some people have been influenced by all the new information available about sexual problems and their solutions. And at the same time, so many problems have been exacerbated by those who have been made most consciously aware of sexual *techniques*.

I have avoided reading most of the treatises myself, and I realize now that if I have come to a better and more sympathetic understanding of the relationship between the sexes, it is not because I studied any new techniques, but because Jerry and I struggled so hard to understand our *feelings*—our own and each other's.

I remember feeling so threatened by impotence during our early years of marriage; it meant only one thing to me— that my worst fears were true, that I was ugly and undesirable; I drowned in self-pity. I never really allowed myself to think about what a nightmare life Jerry was living, how unaware he was of how depressed he felt, how angry and despairing because I demanded so much from him.

It was strange, while talking to Catherine, to realize that impotence could never threaten me now. All it would mean is that there was some hidden agenda of anxiety or sadness, or perhaps even some resentment of my expectations and demands, and that all of these could be surmounted by tenderness and a little creative initiative in lovemaking! I guess the most important thing is that I no longer see it as an attack on me.

I sometimes wonder which is worse anyway, the man who expresses his emotional problems through impotence, or the one who becomes a compulsive stud—boasting of conquest after conquest, who has to spend almost every night with a different woman. Both men are anxious and unsure, angry, unable to allow lovingness to express itself in sex. It seems to me that men who are compulsive about sex tend to be less likely to want to examine their lives. They settle for the surface of life, letting the world know how marvelous they are. Men who are impotent, who suffer from a numbing of their sexual drives, probably suffer so much more that they are more inclined to be willing to face the psychological origins of their difficulties and go through the process of introspection and self-exploration needed.

I wonder if I am more philosophical because I am now older. Could I have been so accepting at the age of twenty-five, even if I had known what I know now and had had better feelings about myself? There is no way to be sure, but I cannot imagine ever behaving as I did, now that I understand how *Jerry* was suffering.

I don't feel guilty any more; I don't blame myself for being young, ignorant, insecure. I guess I feel sorry that instead of trying to help Jerry, I remember most of all getting up at night, sitting at a window, gazing out at a tree or the street, and crying *for myself*. If only we had been able to cry *for each other*, together.

We did try to help each other—we both went into therapy and stuck with it for long periods of time. We also stayed very much in love and supported each other's lives in hundreds of other ways. But it is good to know how far we have come from the ways in which we also tortured ourselves and each other. And nothing brought it home more clearly than Catherine's saying, "He couldn't perform." I cringe at the expression; it isolates people from each other, and means that each suffers unbearable pain alone.

⌒ ELEVEN

It is so strange; we seem to have come full circle. This morning I woke up very early and went into the living room to do some work. I felt marvelously awake and alive—full of creative energy—very much my own person.

About two hours later, Jerry appeared—looking sleepy and sad. I didn't realize anything was wrong, greeted him cheerily and went back to my work. He just stood there. And then he whispered, "Do you love me?" It was said with real anxiety. I felt such a wave of empathy and compassion. I got up and put my arms around him. He held onto me and said, "Sometimes I get frightened. You seem to go so far away." He told me that he had awakened, found me gone, had a sudden feeling of foreboding. Suppose I wanted to get away from him? Suppose I didn't want to come back?

I asked him why he hadn't come to find me sooner. "I didn't want to disturb you," he said, "And I was scared that even if you came back to bed with me, you might not really want to." I promised to tell him how I really felt. "We've tried being polite and protective, and you know where *that* got us!" I said.

I realized his need was important right then—took priority over my privacy, my need to work. I also recognized that part of me wanted to escape, feels frightened that my wings are being clipped. We talked about it; I made him a good breakfast, told him many times how much I loved him and that we would belong together all our lives. It is such a strange new role for me! We talked about all the changes. "You are the one who forced me to grow," I remind him. "If I am more independent, if I need time to be alone, it's all your creation!" He says he's glad—and I say that now he is the one who must be brave. He says, "There was no question of choice, so there is no courage involved. No matter what happens, I want you to be yourself, live your own life. It has to be that way." I keep quiet, but I know how right he is.

⌒ *TWELVE*

What a beautiful day today has been! The first really warm spring day—suddenly there is the first miraculous feeling of GREEN in the park. Jerry called me from his office and suggested we take a half hour off for a walk in the park. It felt illicit and naughty—we both have so much work to do right now. He assured me we'd work much more quickly and efficiently if we took a break. He quoted Santayana at me. Apparently he'd been in the midst of a philosophy lecture when suddenly he'd looked out the window and said, "Pardon me, gentlemen; I have an appointment with April," and walked out of the room!

We were walking hand in hand in the park when a friend waved to us from his bicycle. A few minutes later a woman who had once been a neighbor caught up with us. Without thinking, I said to Jerry, after she'd gone on, "Gee, it's impossible to have an affair in New York! All we're doing is playing hooky, and we keep meeting people we know!" We both laughed—but not comfortably!

It was a lovely interlude. We sat near the lake, eating hot dogs, and Jerry talked more than he has in some time about his feelings. I guess I haven't encouraged him to do so lately. We talked about the fine balance between dependency and freedom. Jerry's attitude is quite clear: one's first loyalty and obligation is to one's marriage partner; that relationship always comes first. But there are always other secondary relationships of many kinds.

An impulsive moment like this—just quitting work and going out to play for a few hours—is so refreshing. Maybe the same thing is necessary in a long marriage. We stopped working today in order to refresh ourselves—get away from dull routines. The work was still there, we really love what we do, and there was no question that we would get back to it. Marriage may be the same thing. I have to admit that there are times when I am somewhat bored with our sexual relationship; we know each other so well—there are few surprises any more. There are variations on the theme—but the theme stays the same. Jerry is an exciting, attractive man. I'd rather spend time with him than with anyone else I know—but there are times now when I have allowed myself to have romantic fantasies about strangers! Jerry must get bored with me, too. It's not that we don't love each other, and sometimes sex is more exciting and more fun than it was twenty years ago—but there are, I guess, limits to how exciting it can be, exclusively, forever. It wouldn't matter if we were younger, or more handsome and beautiful, or knew more "tricks." It's just knowing each other so well; you just can't avoid a certain inevitable predictability. I guess I've never admitted that to myself before!

I have made Jerry too much the center of my universe; I haven't allowed any other relationships to matter to any important degree—especially other men. I have always had wonderful women friends—but how close have I ever allowed myself to get to other men? I work with men all the time. I wonder if any of them would be more interested in me if I showed any interest in them? I have never really allowed myself to find out. Come to think of it, I have never let myself enjoy being with men as much as I have enjoyed my women friends. I cut myself off from other people: I have centered my whole existence around one man. No wonder he has felt caged. But I've been caging myself as well! A scary idea.

〜 *THIRTEEN*

I've been feeling very confused and upset this past week. All I seem to be thinking about is Jerry: where he is, what he is doing. I miss him during the day when I'm working; I hate it when he's out in the evening. It has nothing to do with fear or jealousy—I know there is no one else. I just feel so dependent on him—and so happy when we are together.

I didn't underestand it at all. I thought I'd gotten over that kind of relationship with him. When I described it to Eve, she grinned at me. "I suppose you'll throw something at me," she said. "But it sounds to me as if you're falling in love."

At first I couldn't figure out what she meant. And then, suddenly, it seemed perfectly logical. Of course! Jerry and I have both changed so much that in some ways we have become almost strangers; we have to fall in love with each other all over again. For a few moments, the regrets sweep through me—the might-have-beens. If only we could have been these new selves the first time we fell in love—how different that time would have been. But then, Eve and I went on to talk about NOW. Jerry and I are like a young couple just falling in love. I suppose that if both partners in a marriage really keep on working at self-discovery and never settling for where they are, this kind of rediscovery of each other can go on and on. How interesting!

Where do I seem to be right now in my feelings? I seem to be feeling very, very married! These last few days I have had such an absolute and irrevocable feeling about that—that there is something inevitable about our being married. Jerry's mother's visit accentuated this for me—a sense of our long history, all the things we have lived through, experienced, understood about each other—and most of all *the struggle*—no two people in the world ever worked harder at loving and growing, or were ever more *for* each other at the deepest level. The more I felt this, the more it seemed possible to accept whatever else was also true: that no other relationship could really threaten this central one, and that while there would always be pain and jealousy if there was someone else, it would be endurable pain—I could surmount it, survive it, accept it.

There are different levels of being married. For some, it is necessary for the spouse who is having an affair to protect his partner's feelings and keep it secret; both need it that way. The marriage is just not so inevitable, so necessary, and it could be shaken with feelings of insecurity, loss of self-esteem, etc. Then there is our kind of marriage, where the worst part of any affair is the deceit. *I think we can now survive anything that comes to us as long as we don't try to deceive each other.* That eroded the deep compassion and the trust. It would probably hurt like hell, but whatever comes must be faced together.

We have both used this experience, this crisis, for change, for better communication, for shifting of roles to a better balance. We have hurt each other terribly, but we have never understood each other better or cared more deeply for the other's life. And most of all, we have cared more *for our own* lives, which is at the heart of the matter.

If you feel absolutely certain of being loved, and married-in-the-soul, then you can endure the pain of allowing the other person to experience himself in every way he can; you just can't deprive him. But first you have to come to this feeling of being married, of being alive, of being yourself—and then all else becomes secondary.

Could I have endured it if the affair had continued? I don't really know for sure, but I think I could—now. I feel that Jerry and I are at the center of each other's lives, and that I will believe that from now on; something in me has made that belief truly possible. I will have bad times, but I will know that I am stronger than those moments. We are so truly husband and wife, and I find that there is something about this knowledge that takes away the compulsive pre-occupation with the danger from other people—even other loves.

Eve feels glad when women are attracted to Greg. She says they only love each other more because every day they make the free choice to be together. She feels she is more lovable, not less, because in spite of other relationships, she is the one Greg chooses to come back to.

The subject came up when she mentioned a conference she was planning to attend for a few days. Greg hadn't decided whether or not to go with her; he was afraid he'd cramp her style! Suppose she met someone and wanted to be free for a few days? Are they both crazy? Aren't they playing with fire? Suppose in this free relationship one or the other partner gets *really* involved? I suppose the answer to that would be, then it had to happen anyway. And maybe the freedom to re-choose enhances the marriage relationship, making another profound love relationship less likely. I just don't know *what* I think any more. I only know that I have a sense of flowing—like a river—just moving along inexorably, beginning more and more to feel an anticipation, a curiosity about what may appear around the next bend.

This morning Jerry and I were talking about ourselves and several other marriages of friends—where we think there may be serious problems. I told Jerry that finally I find there are whole days—even a week here and there—when I *really* never think about his affair. He said, "I know it hurt you terribly, but the other relationship really wasn't that important."

It occurs to me that I projected *my* personality onto Jerry's experience. Because of my nature, I had to assume that if he was having an affair it had to be a Grand Passion; that's the only way it could happen to me. I feel so intensely— love so whole-ly. I never stopped to think about the fact that Jerry was more capable of superficial relationships than I. Or if not that exactly, less intense, less emotionally involving ones. He has always been more private, needing other people less, giving less of himself. Why didn't I ever think of that? I guess I've suffered more than I needed to in terms of the objective reality of just how much his involement was. But I don't regret it; suffering this much has taught me more than I could have learned if I had treated it more lightly!

The more I love without resentment and demands, the more Jerry seems to want to let me know that the affair was not an earthshaking relationship, and that it grew out of needs that had no place else to go.

✑ *FOURTEEN*

Being back in Europe reminds me of the time that has passed, how much we have changed. What I think is the essence of the change is that there is no longer any barbed wire around either one of us.

The other part of it is that neither one of us has to feel feelings for the other one. We *both* miss each other and can talk about it; we *both* feel lonely; we *both* enjoy being alone.

When I left Jerry to come home ahead of him, he looked so sad at the airport. He wants to be reassured that I love him, will miss him. He expresses anxiety about the separation—the fear that I might leave him, go off with someone else. I tell him, "Whatever happens to either of us, it's not the end of the world." He looks startled and upset. How full of irony life is! He forced me to learn this—and now isn't always happy about it!

I heard Jerry give a speech yesterday. Afterward I told him how good it was. For the first time in our entire married life, he said, "I worry so about what you'll think." I couldn't believe it. Jerry says he has always felt that way—but was hardly aware of it himself. Lately he has realized just how terribly important my approval has always been. He was very shy about it, but he told me that if I'm critical he feels terrible, and if I praise him he feels wonderful. "Every time I've ever given a speech when you were in the audience, I have almost died of anxiety—worrying that you might think I was terrible." How deep are the roots of our feelings! What I guess he has been unearthing is the most primitive and early feelings of disapproval of his mother. It was so painful, he just screened it out all these years.

I'm *glad* he had the affair! It helped him to realize how much I love him. And he needed desperately to know that.

We had a strange experience before I left to come back home. We were in a small, crowded restaurant in Paris, where there was a young American couple squeezed in at the table next to ours. We could hardly help but get into conversation with them, but as it turned out they were charming and interesting. I felt strangely drawn to them, and it took me a while to figure out exactly what was going on. They were in their middle twenties, very much in love, and by some strange coincidence were both working in the same fields as Jerry and I: same educational background, similar attitudes, interests, points of view. They were very much of their own times—he long-haired and bearded, she in a long muslin dress, no makeup. They were on a weekend holiday in France. Both doing graduate work in England. They had lived together for two years, been married for a year. They had grown up in much the same places we had.

Suddenly I realized they were really *us* a generation later! Only they were doing the things we regretted not having done ourselves. I whispered to Jerry, "It's like seeing our might-have-beens." Sudden tears started in his eyes, and we held hands tightly for a minute. Later on, we talked about it; the young couple seemed so sound, so "put-together." They knew what they wanted to do, they were adventurous, they talked about their relationship so naturally and easily. It was as if they were our young selves without all our hang-ups: my sexual repression, my timidity, our not having had the wits or the guts to use the G.I. Bill after World War II for study abroad; Jerry's crippled emotional state—without all of that baggage, these are who we might have been. It was some comfort to realize that people like us had really done a much better job of raising children to be free and at home in themselves and the world than our parents had been able to do—or theirs before that. But both of us felt waves of sadness and regret the rest of the evening.

ᚖ *FIFTEEN*

A new book has come out which apparently discusses how to cure impotence in one easy lesson! I have gathered from various newspaper and magazine articles on the new sex technicians—engineers of lovemaking—that the sex clinics have had this secret formula for years now. Every once in a while I have wondered if Jerry and I were crazy not to have investigated this approach, but both of us resisted it violently.

We both feel that the roots of symptoms go so deep—they are so much more than physiology—that if one takes an easy, mechanical route toward solving it, one of two things is likely to happen; either the problem will simply reappear in some new guise—or even worse, at some deep level, one gives up the cry for help that the symptom represented.

Jerry and I discussed this a couple of days ago, when I told him about this new book. Therapy takes so much longer and is so much harder, but what Jerry has been learning about himself—especially these past couple of years—seems so essential, that the symptom becomes far less important than the learning it evokes. Jerry was more open with me than he has ever been before. Actually, it wasn't that so much as his own greater ability to articulate his feelings to *himself*. He says that he has recently been facing feelings of terror and rage that seem quite unbelievable; they are surfacing from the most primitive levels—feelings of being an infant, preverbal feelings, that now must be brought to consciousness and to understanding. He told me, "It's not new ground, but of course, the deeper you go, the more powerful the feelings. I think I'm really feeling it all—or almost all—for the first time. It was a lovely formula: my mother sent me three messages from the time I was born. (1) I should never have been conceived; (2) I should have been a girl—she was repulsed by having to care for a male child; and (3) I ought to solve all of her problems."

It occurs to me that our marital difficulties stem in good part from the degree to which I participated in number three! It also occurs to me that the human mind is a wonderful thing—a thought that comes to consciousness more and more frequently during these years of growing up!

DIALOGUE

ME: You know, it just occurred to me that there is a wonderful wisdom of the unconscious. Even though you have had some level of understanding of these forces before, the rage and terror seem much more real now, as well as your ability to talk about it. Meanwhile, while all this has been going on, your relationship with your mother has steadily improved! It's almost as if you had to work that out in the real world before you could really look at the painful feelings of childhood.

JERRY: You know, you're absolutely right! It would have been impossible to face all this so directly, while she was still able to force me into reacting as if her demands were reasonable. That's how I always felt: not that what she wanted was wrong, but that somehow I ought to be able to give her what she wanted.

ME: And you also couldn't examine it or talk to me about it until our relationship had improved, until I accepted frustration without being threatened or angry. . . .

JERRY: And I could accept impotence as a signal of unfinished business and not as a threat to my masculinity.

ME: Neither of us are crazy about these periods of abstinence, but thank God we are not attacking ourselves or each other any more.

JERRY: Those feelings still emerge, but with less force. I still get feelings of shame. . . .

ME: And I wander into that old place where I feel undesirable—but I just let it happen, I accept it, and it goes away.

JERRY: The good times have certainly been better than ever before. . . .

ME: And as they get better and better, we'll both know we didn't take the easy way out. . . .

JERRY: God no! Believe me, there have been times when the thought of trying hypnosis or conditioning or some other quick panacea seemed very attractive. . . .

ME: Strangely enough, that's never been true for me. This whole business has always been worse for you than for me—maybe that's why I never really thought about any alternative but encouraging you to learn more about yourself. But I hope it was more than that; I hope it was because I wanted you to find out what your body was trying to tell you about your past, your life, your feelings. . . .

JERRY: Have I ever told you that I love you?

✎ *SIXTEEN*

This morning I woke up very early and decided to get up and do some work. Jerry was uncovered, and I walked over to his side of the bed to try to cover him. He was curled up in a fetal position, holding all the covers in his arms. I felt deeply moved. He used to sleep like a rock, on his back— still, defended against the world, even in his sleep. Now he seems so vulnerable, so childlike. I realize how much he is changing, too. We both struggle so hard to break down the barriers of fear, to risk feeling more alive.

I have always been able to return to childhood, to play at being his baby, his little girl. My childhood was so much happier than his. It never frightened me to allow myself the pleasures of regression! It makes me so happy to see him beginning to let go. He has become so much more cuddly! I realize now, when we lie holding each other, that there is a pleasure that is new, a kind of softness to his body, a melting and blending. The hard edges are disappearing, the stiffening against contact comes less and less frequently.

It suddenly occurs to me that the softer he becomes all over, the stiffer he can be at the appropriate moments in the appropriate parts! I am shocked at myself! But not very.

⌒SEVENTEEN

Jerry is leaving this evening on a five-week trip—half business, half pleasure. For the past few days he's been mentioning the name of a woman. I paid no attention the first few times, but this morning he said something about having given her address as a central place where he could be reached—that he would keep in touch with her about his exact whereabouts. I began hearing and wondering. He met her about two years ago on a similar trip. I gather she's a woman in her fifties, and very accomplished. Jerry obviously likes and admires her.

Teasing, I said, "Now listen! Just remember—it's OK for a few days, but don't get too involved!" Jerry looked at me in wonder and delight. It is hard for both of us to believe I am the same woman who screamed divorce and/or suicide a short while ago.

I had a busy day, but late this afternoon, coming home in a cab, I began thinking about how I would really feel if this was a Relationship coming up. Jealous—but quietly; refusing to be totally shut out; and sure that Jerry would tell me. And then, like a flash—a thought came that warmed my soul and made me want to shout out, sing a song, dance a little jig. The thought was: if Jerry doesn't come back to me, he's a damned fool; I'm the best he could ever find and the best for him. *Wow!* I could hardly believe what I was thinking and feeling—but I know it's real and no game, no rationalization. *I really do believe*, for the first time in my life, that I am something very special, lovable, fascinating, full of life, talented—any man who'd give me up would be an idiot! There is a deep sense of peace, homecoming—to myself. I am cherished—by myself most of all. I wept there in the taxi, with joy.

ᕐᗌ *EIGHTEEN*

Jerry just left on his trip. We lay quietly in bed for an hour until it was time for him to leave for the airport. We tried to nap, holding each other close, but I felt myself pulling away, getting ready to let him go, trying not to show my sadness. Jerry felt it almost at once. He said, "You're leaving me. It's frightening—like an emptiness in my arms." I tried to explain that it was partly my fear that I would behave badly as I used to, that I would cling and he would feel guilty and then angry. He assured me it wasn't like that any more. We are both sad, and if I feel like saying, "Don't leave me," or if I cried, that would be all right. It wouldn't be a demand or helplessness—it would just be the simple fact that we both feel sad.

When he left we both cried. "It's crazy," he said. "We've been married almost thirty years—how can we still feel this way?" And then he corrected himself: "*have come* to feel this way."

"We've earned it," I said. "Nobody ever worked harder for this kind of loving."

Jerry said, "I'm finding out that geography is no longer relevant!" What he meant was that getting ready to leave on this trip had made him realize that he doesn't need to make this declaration of freedom any more; he can be just as free at home. In addition, since he is now far more able to experience his own feelings without a great deal of repression going on, he misses me and can acknowledge it. "Well," he said, resignedly, "this is another learning experience."

It still seems incredible, but I remember very well how I used to behave when he went away, even on a business trip. First of all I was always in a rage because he could dare to leave me—and even worse, seem to be glad about it. I was such a clinger; looking back, it seems more appropriate to say I was a jailer. I was so frightened by any indication that he didn't need to be with me every second of his life. That idea was terribly threatening because it affirmed my feelings about myself—that there was really no good reason why anyone would *want* to be with me.

I cried before, during, and after such "escapes." I sure made Jerry pay for them! On several of his longer trips, I wrote him about every catastrophe that was going on at home, to punish him for being away. He must have loved me so much to have tolerated me! How terrible it must have been to be seeing some wonders of the world, trying to have his own special adventures, while being forced to feel guilty and worried because of my anger and dependence —my unwillingness to let go. It is really a wonder that he *ever* came back—and that in the midst of feeling so imprisoned by my needs, he turned to only one other woman.

Which is an interesting thought, as a matter of fact. When Jerry sounds so lonely—he even asked if he should come home sooner and give up part of his trip—I find *myself* beginning to feel uneasy. I *want* this time alone, but even more than that, his loving me so much right now begins to feel like a burden sometimes and makes *me* want to be free —for other relationships, myself!

How amazing it is when marriage partners grow and change so much that they shift roles almost completely! It certainly helps one to understand how the other one has felt. It is no longer a matter of Jerry explaining or telling me that freedom makes love deeper; I know it through what I am now experiencing myself.

It occurs to me that part of Jerry's gloom this past week has been his mourning for an old neurosis. We get so used to the sick parts of ourselves, and it is so painful to give them up! I think that Jerry was discovering that it was no longer necessary to run away to feel free, and that must have been a strange and frightening discovery in some ways. We talked about it briefly a few days ago when he came down with a cold. I told him I thought maybe his cold was a kind of crying for a part of himself that no longer existed. He agreed and told me, "You know, that's really interesting. Yesterday I had lunch with George, who has just finished a new book. Apparently part of it has to do with the struggles we go through when we try to change ourselves. He told me he'd had a lot of trouble with his digestive system for years, any time he was tense or upset. A couple of months ago he went through some really terrible traumas—and his stomach didn't act up at all. Part of him felt very bereft! It's hard to adjust to the loss of a nice, comfortable, familiar neurotic symptom!"

Following this discussion of feeling grief for lost parts of oneself, I spent the weekend with Annie. At one point she was talking about how much she would like to remarry, eventually, but her manner was quiet, soft, thoughtful. I said, "I think it will happen sooner now, because you have changed so much." She looked puzzled, and then I explained by demonstrating—imitating her. Six months ago, her voice would have been strident, her movements sharp and jerky, her tone and words full of impatience, resentment. Then I imitated the way she had just been talking—slower movements of her hands, quietness in her face. She looked shocked. Later I realized it was dumb as hell to have brought her attention to the change that was going on, for all the rest of the weekend she was her "old self"—strident, restless —something hard and tough in her voice. At first I couldn't figure out what in hell had happened. Then, after thinking about Jerry's experiences, it dawned on me. I had reminded Annie that she was growing, changing—and in a kind of grief reaction, she reverted to her old self! You don't give up parts of yourself, however neurotic, without some sense of loss.

A BIRTHDAY LETTER TO MYSELF

Dear Me:

I think you're doing fine! You are more a woman and more yourself than you have ever been. I'm proud of how you have met life head-on—hesitating and halting only when demon fears from deep inside kept you paralyzed—never from a conscious choice to hide.

I *like* you! I take for granted that you know I approve of your work and your relationships with co-workers and friends—but I've always approved of that. What I like most, now, are new things, like:

1. You stop to think something over carefully, after the spontaneous instinct. You talk to yourself about decisions, and give yourself time to study the feelings that eventually float to the surface.

2. You don't need any more to tell Jerry everything you are thinking and feeling.

3. You can lean on other people—men especially,

since you've almost never done that before. It feels good.

4. You have separated yourself from the demands of people you love at a profound level that is quite secret and awesome. You care a lot, and you have a sense of responsibility, but deep down you feel free of their wants.

5. *You can take care of yourself!!!!!!* How marvelous to know that Jerry's necessities for freedom and pirvacy no longer leave you destitute, that you are a nourisher of your own soul, a watching guard, on duty day and night to care for yourself. And very well.

I have no idea what will happen to you. I don't think there is any reason to think about that really. Life was always absolutely uncertain, there were never any promises; you just didn't understand that. But it seems likely that you can now find your way home to yourself, whatever is going on.

I suppose the more remarkable (and still mostly inarticulate) change I sense is the way liking the person you are spreads into all the nooks and crannies of self-distaste—even the oldest and toughest of them, like how you look. I feel a warm glow creeping through me—an acceptance of my face and body—that I am alive and human and beautiful in my own way. I feel at peace at an inner level, deep below the turmoil of life. I want to stay with you always,

Love,
Me

ᘓ *NINETEEN*

Jerry just came back from his trip. He looks more tired than when he left, and was more eager and ready to come home than I was to have him here.

It is really amazing how much I've come to enjoy my own company—and utter solitude. When I come into a silent, empty apartment, I no longer think of it as empty. It is full of *me* when I walk in! I love the freedom of choice: to eat when I'm hungry, sleep when I'm tired, work or goof off, be wonderfully efficient and do a million chores, working through the night—or spend a delicious, sinful day in bed watching dumb television programs. You don't have to consider anyone else's needs when you are alone, and what that does is force you to be more in touch with your own needs and wishes. I now find it not only refreshing but necessary. Usually by the time Jerry and I return to each other, I'm more than ready. This time his need of me was greater, and it made me realize how much we have changed.

Now there are moments when I feel itchy, uneasy, straining at the leash of his dependence on me; for the first time I can understand how he must have felt when I was doing that to him, all the time. We are both in the process of learning how to touch and how to release, how to encourage and support and how to leave each other alone.

⌒ *TWENTY*

This morning I was crossing the street when a strange man took my arm very firmly and started walking with me. I was startled and frightened—and then confused when he said, "I know who you are, Jo, even if you don't know me." Apparently he knew me through my work and had seen me a few times before in another city, but we'd never been introduced. He wanted to take me for a cup of coffee; he said he was a great admirer of mine; he told me I was "a wonderful-looking woman!" He asked about my marital status, invited me to the theater. I thanked him, told him I was meeting my husband, and as I rounded a corner he shouted, "Listen! I'd love to get to know you! If you change your mind, I'm in room 1505 at the Roosevelt Hotel!"

At one time I would have jumped and run like a scared rabbit—maybe even looked for a policeman. Today I was both amused and flattered. I have to look into this mirror of myself as men see me; it happens too often now to be accidental. Something in me has changed radically; I send out different messages. I am no longer defended against friendship with men. I'M CRAZY ABOUT MEN! I must be letting them know it, by some unconscious shift in body language and attitude.

When I told this incident to Jerry, he made an interesting observation. He was at a meeting when I spoke several weeks ago. At the end of the meeting a number of people wanted to talk to me personally. Jerry said, "I've seen you in that situation many times, but usually it was mostly women who

came to talk to you, to tell you how much they love you.
This time I noticed it was almost all men—and you were
flirting with them! I loved it!" He's absolutely right! This *is*
a new phenomenon. It reminds me of adolescence, when all
the girls feel like wallflowers and all the boys are scared to
death—but neither understands how the others are feeling.
By changing myself—feeling more self-confident and therefore being able to feel more compassion for others—I find
myself understanding for the first time that *men* suffer,
that they want to be liked—loved, that they are desperate
for approval and acceptance, *they need me!* Men are as shy,
as frightened, as afraid of being alone, as needful of loving
as I have ever been. I'm ashamed of what a slow learner
I am!

ꙮ TWENTY-ONE

It is New Year's Eve, and I suddenly realize with a great
sense of shock that it's been more than *two years* since I
started this diary! It would be impossible to believe that so
much time has passed if it were not for the fact that this
person who is myself seems to be someone so different. I
remember how I felt and how I acted in the beginning, but
feel a strange sense of disassociation; I can understand how
that poor creature felt, but know that she has disappeared,
gone forever, and left me here instead. There is some pain
in this. Whether or not one likes the selves that one slowly
discards in the process of growing, they were still one's own.
I don't want that hysterical child to come back—but I have
to admit that I mourn her as someone I knew who has died.

As I began recalling the events of these years, I was also shocked to realize how few facts I really know about the affair. Almost everything I've written about it is surmise—invention, imagination, very often what I needed to believe. It infuriates me that Jerry remains so private, so close-mouthed—and yet it also comforts me in one sense, because it is clear that he would never have talked to Nina about me. It is just not his nature. I can't imagine being able to separate two parts of my life that way. With me, everything spills in all directions; if anything important is happening to me, I have a great need to share it with him. I suppose that's one reason why I'm sure I could never fall in love with someone else or have an affair, certainly not while I love Jerry and want to live with him.

What do I really know? I saw Nina once, so long ago that I have only the vaguest impression of her. I know she has had periods of distress about work and lovers, and that she was dependent on Jerry for advice, comfort. I know that she made the initial overtures and that he was surprised at first. I have no idea how intense the relationship was after it began; I have no idea how often they saw each other, how often they made love. I know he must have enjoyed the relationship because it went on for several years; I don't know whether it was two years or three—or even more— Jerry was very vague about it—but I have often wondered if he told me it was a shorter period of time than it really was. I am not sure how it ended. I have no idea what they talked about, what other kinds of needs each fulfilled for the other, other than those few things Jerry and I have had to talk about. Most of all, I haven't any idea, really, of what she is like, what she felt during and after the affair.

And I know I will never know any more than I do now. Jerry stiffens and becomes unhappy if I ask the most casual question, trying to define the affair in some way, learn about it. He will never *want* to tell me anything, and I will never force any such issue.

But despite this lack of facts, my life has changed incredibly. This mysterious relationship, with all its factual unknowns, has been the catalyst for more growth and change in me than anything that has ever happened to me before. It may have been *his* private affair, but it sure as hell has been *my* life!

I suppose the most important change in me is that I understand unconditional love. I am not always capable of giving it, but I become so more and more all the time. To love with an open hand, not to try to own another human being, to leave necessary spaces between us so that each of us can become more and more ourselves, separately. It is slow and painful, but now there are times when I am actually glad when we are separated for a few days—even for a few weeks. The companion I am finding inside myself becomes more and more satisfying. I still have awful days—the black abyss of emptiness—but it lasts a shorter time each time I am really by myself.

The most important learning for both of us is that I will no longer carry the burden of expressing Jerry's emotions for him! As I see him changing—getting in touch with his feelings at the moment he has them, not six months later! —I marvel at what a heavy load I used to carry. Having to be sad for both of us when we were apart, having to be angry for both of us when someone did something awful to him, being afraid and threatened the times when Julie seemed to be in trouble—God knows I carried all the guilt and self-condemnation!

I suppose this is one of the most interesting things I've learned about marriage, because I understood it the least before. Almost—or even completely—unconsciously, one partner tends to assign strong feelings, certain behaviors, to the other. Rather than both partners sometimes having certain kinds of feelings and sharing them, the more emotional, expressive person does the psychological work for both. I see this, for example, in my father since my mother died. We used to think that she was the one who could be very critical of a great many people, who worried ridiculously when one of us was flying, who set very high standards for her grandchildren and demanded a great deal from them. When she died, we discovered much to our surprise that our father behaved in just those ways, where before he had appeared to be quite passive in these situations. He had let my mother do all the expressing for both of them; what a burden that was for her! I saw the same thing again recently when a friend died. He was a very funny man—a professional comedian. Whenever we were with him, he was "on," entertaining all the time. His wife laughed at him with all the rest of us —really loved his jokes. We always thought she was a mousy, colorless person. After he died, we discovered much to our surprise that she was funny as hell herself. In this case, one can see how deprived the "silent partner" can be. Jerry and I understand that now, too. I carried the burden of expressing our emotions for both of us—but he was malnourished emotionally by letting me do that. As I watch him learn to express love, hate, sadness, loneliness—even worry and fear—I see him grow; his personality becomes bigger, stronger. He is enriched by what he feels—he is so much more alive and human.

After a while I am sure it will become less conscious on both our parts. Now when we *both* can cry about something, we feel astonished and terribly pleased about it! When you share feelings this way, you feel a closeness that is never possible otherwise.

I just had a frightening thought; if all this has happened to me in a couple of years, what lies ahead in the next few years? What a scary idea! But how exciting, too.

༰ *TWENTY-TWO*

Love is very simple; you just give it. That's all.

Beginning

*T*oday was one of those luscious Sundays. Jerry and I close and loving—a long dalliance abed—late enough for me to be really awake, thank you, and so to lovely lovemaking. Then a walk in the park, a ride on the carousel, peanuts for the squirrels, quiet talking about Jerry's work, my wonderings about what I want to do next. I feel shy about some of my thoughts, but Jerry is immediately enthusiastic, encouraging. We sit on a park bench to rest. It is now almost three years of this newness in who we are with each other. All the growing, all the sense of loving more and not owning each other. Laughing, I suddenly say, "Gee—I'm getting nervous! Things have been so great between us, so comfortable and open and good. I've been on a sort of emotional plateau for a few months—it's the first time in years! It's scary. I wonder what will happen next?" Jerry laughs, too. "Uh, oh," he says. "That sounds like 'Here We Go Again' coming up!"

We stop for a pizza to take home for supper. Companionably, we work separately for a couple of hours. I feel loved and safe and contented.

❦

Jerry is on a business trip—will be away for several weeks. I miss him. Last night I had dinner with Peter. I hadn't seen him since his divorce, and he suddenly called about a week ago. I told him it was providential—I needed company. We had worked together for several years and had had a mild flirtation—both feeling safely and happily married (my God, how much has happened to us both since then!), and therefore able to enjoy a kind of game of indecent propositioning of each other. I remember once we'd been at a public meeting, sitting next to each other on a dais, and while appearing to be upstanding, serious, hardworking, co-professionals, we had actually been discussing plans for a sinful encounter! He had always made me feel attractive and feminine, and I thought dinner might be an adventure.

It was awful. Peter was deeply depressed, almost entirely out of contact with me. There was no joy in our meeting, and after telling me some of his troubles, he seemed bored. In the past he had always greeted me with a shout of glee and a big hug; this time, even though we hadn't seen each other for about a year, he hardly seemed to notice me at all. It was a lousy evening, and I came home feeling sorry for him and even sorrier for my poor lonely self.

The next day Jerry called. He asked about the dinner, and I told him it was depressing; I'd felt rejected. Jerry was sorry. We agreed we were both tired of this separation—had slept alone enough nights, wished his trip was over. Then, without thinking, I said, "Listen—maybe you'll have better luck than I had!" Jerry began to scream with laughter—great, earthy, hearty yelling, coast to coast! Sometimes I say things that shock me into realizing how much I have changed. Imagine! *Me* kidding about *that!* I try to imagine something like that happening five years ago. Even to joke about such a thing would have shocked, even horrified me.

I realize we are so close now that we could even share pieces of our lives that would in some ways be unsharable. I said, "Peter made me feel like an old maiden aunt—an Edna Mae Oliver type. Comfort me—tell me I'm cute and sexy." Jerry obliged with great enthusiasm. I felt glad I'd made him laugh, that we'd been able to have this kind of joke with each other. I like myself so much better the way I am now. This telephone conversation made me feel less lonely; Jerry was still gone, but I had myself for company again. When I feel good about myself, I am not alone.

Millie and Arthur just stayed with us for a few days. Yesterday Arthur left for Boston; today Millie is flying to Miami to visit her mother. They will meet back at home in Arizona in about five days.

Last night I started to ask Millie how come Arthur hadn't called her before she left on the next part of her trip, and then I caught myself; it was none of my business. What startled me, though, was the realization that once upon a time Jerry would have behaved exactly as Arthur had. I would have felt uneasy and isolated, but Jerry would have been practical and sensible and would have assured me that as long as we could reach each other in case of emergency, why should we call? I suddenly realized that the way things are between us now, *Jerry* would *need* to call *me*. He would have called last night to tell me about his business in Boston; he would have called this morning to say good-bye before I left for Miami; he would have called me in Miami tonight to make sure I'd arrived safely. His ability to get in touch with his love-anxiety feelings has certainly been a boon to the telephone company!

I found myself feeling sorry for Millie—although she

seemed perfectly comfortable to be out of touch with Arthur for these few days. Each couple has to find their own rhythm —but I was more sharply aware of how much I enjoy Jerry's lovingly protective ways. And of course it isn't only a change in him. It is also true that I no longer feel I have a God-given right to such attentions, and I don't ask for them. I can accept my own feelings and allow Jerry to behave in response to his needs. With the freedom to choose, he has been able to give so much more!

Jerry is out of town. I met Martin at the cleaner's this morning, and he asked what I was doing for dinner. I'd turned down two dinner invitations because I was really enjoying being alone after several weeks of wall-to-wall people.

I've met Martin a number of times over the past few years, and we've talked about many things, but never had a "date." I knew his divorce had gone through about three months ago and that he'd taken an apartment in our neighborhood. He's a fascinating and talented man who has overcome horrendous problems. He has always been charming and gallant when we met—full of compliments and appreciation—and I thought the idea of our having dinner together delightful! It was—animated, gay, warmly affectionate. I felt stimulated intellectually and greatly appreciated as a woman. He's a touchy-feely man—a hand-holder, a hugger. There was nothing really provocative about it—although I had the feeling that would have been perfectly possible if I had encouraged it. We had dinner at a neighborhood restaurant and then he walked me home, came upstairs, and we had some coffee. He told me that he had shared pieces of his life with me that he had not talked to anyone else about. I was very touched and said so. With tears in his eyes he said shyly, "I think I have loved you for some time." I told him the feeling was mutual and hugged him.

What is so remarkable is that I *allowed him to care for me*. I wasn't afraid of being rejected; I wasn't afraid of letting myself feel loving toward him. And perhaps most important of all, I knew that I was in control of my own life and would make my own decisions—not be swept away into doing anything I might regret. I can't really think of anything I could regret very much (unless it involved hurting someone) because I learn *so much* from everything that happens to me.

Walking home, I told Martin I had to get to bed early—I'd had a long day and a lot to do tomorrow. He said, "Never fear. I'll stay a few minutes and then I'll tuck you in." The light changed and we began to cross the street. I hadn't answered, and I think he was worried that he'd said the wrong thing. "Don't get nervous," he said, "I meant your own bed, alone." I replied, "Why should I be nervous? I only do the things I want to do." Now that I think about it, I never believed that when I was young. I feel bathed in a warm, soft light of loving feelings. There is no longer a sense of great danger.

After Martin left, I was full of renewed surprise and wonder at the woman I have become. Five years ago I could never have allowed myself such a pleasant encounter. I know that these years of change have helped me immeasurably to see myself as a desirable, interesting, attractive woman, worthy of being loved in many ways. How it enriches my life! The more I am able to take risks, the more I find there is no risk at all—only new experiences, new learnings—more loving. I fell asleep quietly, happily—and gratefully.

᠊ᓭᕋ

Sometimes I have the feeling that I have lost control of the speed of learning and am on some sort of roller coaster that can only lead to a disastrous collision at the end of the ride. I've learned so many things these last few years—opened myself up to so much growing—and today I want desperately to STOP for a while—rest—but it seems too late; I go on risking new perceptions, new feelings, whether I want to or not.

What brought on these thoughts at this particular moment is Martin. We have had dinner together several times now. He is a charming, talented, intelligent man, and our discussions are animated, exciting. We stimulate each other intellectually—but what came as a great shock to me is that the stimulation is far more general than that. And we both know it.

I keep hearing a long-ago parental voice in the background, telling me that sex and love must always go together! I have known intellectually for a long time that this was nonsense, but I have managed to avoid direct emotional confrontation with this issue until now. I am not in love with Martin, but he is an attractive man, and the thought of going to bed with him is exciting. I begin to crawl back into my childhood terrors of being a fallen woman, while Eve keeps assuring me that one can have all one's feelings and still make choices. I understand that; but I think my choices are all going to be wanton! What *is* becoming of me? Where is that proper, repressed, middle-aged lady disappearing to? I feel nervous, unsettled—and about fifteen years old. Or rather, how I ought to have felt then.

෴

It occurred to me last night that the most important thing I've learned in these past few fascinating, agonizing, adventurous years is that a Passion for Life is what living and growing are all about, and that this kind of passion takes many forms—sex being only one part of it. In the revolution between total repression and total permissiveness, the importance of sex has become disproportionate to its real significance in life. It can be full of joy and wonder and pleasure, but the passion that gives life meaning is far broader than that.

Last night there was a program on television—about Eleanor Roosevelt. Watching the development of that beautiful woman, that most human of all human beings, I suddenly realized that *she* had more passion for life than any of the people who are now trying all the variety of novel ways of expressing themselves through sex. Repressed, inhibited (which contributed to her own tragic suffering, ultimately), she exulted in living, risked everything, every day, allowed herself to be real and vulnerable, to *care*—probably more than almost anyone else has ever cared—about the human race.

I began to feel ashamed of this diary; there is so much preoccupation with the small and intimate feelings—it seems so egocentric, narcissistic—so preoccupied with the personal.

And yet, as I think about it, I am surprised to realize how much my personal voyage has affected other people. I have helped more friends, more strangers, than ever before in my life; I never cared more about children, about growing, about helping people to realize life while they are living it. That line from *Our Town* seems to have become a theme in all my messages to the world, in everything I do.

At work today Ken told me that his wife had said something interesting about me. I met her once briefly about three years ago. Last week we met again at the theater. She told Ken that I looked softer and younger now than I had then. Ken told me, "Ruth said there was such humanity shining in your face! She's right. I realized that of all the people we work with, you are the most loved."

I was close to tears. Not merely touched—it was more than that. I think it was a new step in growing: to know that when one pursues the personal quest, when one struggles not to be afraid, to welcome life and to hold out one's arms lovingly to others, something happens inside that makes one more than one has ever dared to be before. I think I have become infectious with health! I see it in the eyes of people who talk to me, in letters I get, sometimes from people I know only slightly. It is as if I have become a Pied Piper for grown-ups—that in the brave act of deciding for life, I have teased and enticed others into following this same dangerous and necessary route toward becoming all one can be. That is the essence of passion; it is surely what being human and alive is all about.

It isn't the act of sex that needs so much discussion, examination, experimentation—it is our *ideas* about *loving*. In a way, this diary is the exact opposite of a sex manual! For me it has become a manual of ideas and feelings about loving.

One day I was having lunch with two men who have been close friends for some time. One of them was involved in several love affairs simultaneously and wanted our opinions on the difference between a strong sexual attraction and falling in love. The other man said, "Love is where, looking back, you can hardly remember exactly when sex started." That's an oversimplification, of course, but I think it helps to clarify the relationship of sex to loving.

The current preoccupation with sexual techniques seems

to me to reflect the absence of introspection. If Jerry and I had refused to examine the inner core of what we felt about ourselves and each other all during our lives together, it is conceivable that each of us might have gone off into a frenzied search for comfort in kicks, in momentary excitement of some kind. Inner despair is a kind of crossroad; you can search for its causes and move toward living and loving, or you can deny its existence and end up having tried every sexual position and "trick" in a never-ending search for some elusive fulfillment that never comes. If we had been different people, less inclined toward the inward search, I imagine that we might have concluded that what we both needed was more variety in our sexual lives, and we might have become part of the swinging set. Many beds, many partners—no rainbow at the end of the trail.

What seems to have happened instead is that sex relations with each other have a vitality and a color that improves because we are changing internally.

During my childhood, long before the sexual revolution or women's liberation—or the more general social revolution of our times—it all seemed so simple, so romantic. You grew up, and if you were lucky (and worked at it very hard!), you would meet The Perfect Man, marry, have children— and live happily ever after. Almost all the movies of my childhood *ended* when the couple decided to marry. Problems were all associated with the process of falling in love; the Other Woman, jobs, relatives, misunderstandings, fateful events over which one had little or no control—these made courtships difficult, hazardous; but once there was that final kiss and the couple walked off into the sunset on the screen, my generation concluded that all the rest was gravy; they had it made.

There was almost no discussion during my adolescence of

marriage as a *choice*; it was an inevitability. And monogamy, without adultery, was the name of the game. It was not until I was a grown woman—married myself—that I began to learn about some of the *real* events that were going on during my childhood, from which children were carefully protected. I was shocked to learn that what I had thought were mild flirtations among my parents' contemporaries were actually a helluva lot more; I was appalled.

It was partly the mood of the times—to keep the lid on reality—but more than that, within my own family there was a strong residue of Victorianism. My parents were both virgins when they married, and never faltered in their devotion to each other. It wasn't until after many years of psychotherapy that I began to understand the fine line of distinction between devotion and enslavement.

I have lived through a period of such turmoil, such upheaval; what to believe? How to conduct my own life? *The rules are all gone!* Some people, reading this diary, might disapprove of the freedom we have tried to introduce into our marriage; they will be the ones who grew up when I did and have somehow managed to keep their blinders on. The majority, I think, will feel "Much ado about nothing." In a society of mate-switching and swinging, of massage parlors and nude encounters, of oral sex on the screen and Johnson and Masters in every bedroom, a couple who are struggling to allow each other room for privacy and freedom is strictly Squaredom Revisited.

I guess that what I have been doing is to reexamine sex, love, and marriage without the limitations of my childhood perceptions, to look at my experiences, explore my feelings, and then come to my own adult conclusions. We must never cut ourselves off from that quest—to find out more and more about how to love and be loved. It seems to me that nothing comes closer to being the essence of what it means to be human.

Love is the most serious responsibility of all; it is the capacity for a lifetime of tenderness and compassion which most differentiates us from other animals. Love between a man and a woman seems to me to be the most difficult, the most sensitizing, and the most gratifying of all the experiences that are possible to human beings. In that context, the marriage contract becomes secondary. It is convenient for taxes, life insurance, and the nurturing of the young. Loving is the ultimate testament of what is best in human beings— the highest form of relating.

A few nights ago Jerry and I went to have dinner with Claire and Charlie, ostensibly to celebrate Charlie's twenty-sixth birthday. We hadn't seen them since they asked for our help when they were both having a lot of problems. We recommended that they both get some psychotherapy, and when they called to invite us for dinner, it was primarily to let us know they were grateful for our advice. We had a lovely evening, and Jerry and I were touched by the way they treat each other. Each still has strong feelings of inferiority, and in a gentle and loving way they reassure each other: Charlie praises Claire's cooking; she praises his choice of wine; Claire tells proudly of his accomplishments as a singer; Charlie insists on showing us Claire's latest photographs.

To watch such a relationship is to be involved in the most civilizing force in the world. It is the only thing that can save us from dark despair—and, eventually, killing each other off. *It is so well worth studying!* I guess what I am saying is that what I seem to have been doing in all these notebooks is searching for the ways in which we can learn to love each other more. I couldn't have accomplished anything by wild experimentation, by momentary forgetting in alcohol or drugs, or in promiscuity. I don't believe there is any alternative except the inward journey, the discovery of oneself. And, at least to my own satisfaction, I think I have proven that it works.

❧

There is no putting yesterday away. It happened. I woke up this morning and remembered with a terrible sense of shock and foreboding. I felt as if I wanted to take the whole day and fold it up like a blanket or a piece of clothing and put it in a summer storage box—with camphor! But my feelings of elation and confusion were too strong. One thing seemed absolutely essential; I *had* to talk to Jerry. We sat at the kitchen table, and although the room was quite warm, my teeth were chattering and I was shaking and shivering.

DIALOGUE

ME: Jerry, something very strange happened yesterday, and I have to talk to you about it.

JERRY: I thought something was going on—you seemed all closed up last night.

ME: It has to do with my having lunch with Paul yesterday. We had some work to discuss, but for the first time since we've known each other, he talked about his personal life. He has a terrible marriage—he's very unhappy. . . .

JERRY: I'm really sorry to hear that; I know how much you like him. . . .

ME: You *do*? I didn't know myself. . . .

JERRY: In the past three years, every time you have ever mentioned him to me, it's been to tell me how much you loved working with him, how kind and gentle he is. . . .

ME: That's interesting. I wasn't aware of that. Maybe that's all there is to it—that I've just become conscious of liking him a lot. . . .

JERRY: What happened?

ME: I don't really know. After lunch, we walked back to the office. I heard myself talking very fast, giving him all sorts of practical advice. I felt peculiar, and I realized I was somehow pushing him away by my chatter. You see, at lunch, he didn't just tell me about his troubles. He said he loved me! It was the strangest conversation. . . .

JERRY: What's strange about that?

ME: I'm serious; I think he was sort of hoping that I was as unhappy as he was and might leave you. . . .

JERRY: Are you sure you want to tell me all this?

ME: I have to. . . .

JERRY: I don't mind; it's just that you know I feel you have a right to your own privacy. . . .

ME: Jerry, that's part of the problem. I would never be able to keep secrets from you. And I think we've learned that the only real danger is the loss of trust. When I left Paul, his eyes were so sad I could hardly look at him. Halfway across the street, I was suddenly almost knocked over by such a wave of loving. I haven't felt anything like it for anyone but you. Such caring; his unhappiness seemed unendurable; I wanted desperately to run back, take him in my arms, try to comfort him. . . .

JERRY: I can understand how you felt. . . .

ME: Suppose I fell in love with him? The way I feel right now, I want to see him again—and I can't guarantee that might not happen. I'm terribly scared. But I think for the first time since Nina, I am beginning to understand how you felt. I can't believe it, but right now it feels as if you *can* love two people. . . .

JERRY: [*Tears almost coming*] Darling—don't be afraid. . . .

ME: Are you telling me that it's all right? That you wouldn't be jealous? You wouldn't mind if I loved another man? I don't believe it. Nobody is *that* noble. Or if you wouldn't mind, then I don't see how you could love me. . . .

JERRY: I can't guarantee anything either. I don't know how I would feel. Maybe I'd want to kill you; maybe I'd be miserably unhappy. [*He stands up, towering above me; begins to pace the floor with strong, firm steps.*] But there is one thing you *must* understand: there is only one thing I absolutely could not bear—and that is your denying any part of your life, anything that is part of growing and becoming more. If you were to stop these feelings you're having, in order not to hurt me, I think that would be the end of our marriage.

ME: I love you so much. You're a much better person that I am. You really look glad—as if something good has happened to me. . . .

JERRY: I think it has.

ME: You're right—I can see it; the more you tell me to feel my feelings, live my life, the more I love you. Oh, Jerry! I feel so awful that I behaved like a stupid child, running away from what I felt! There was Paul, risking, letting me know his pain, his love—and what was I doing? Playing the brisk, impersonal amateur social worker. . . .

JERRY: It sounds to me as if you should call him right away and let him know how you really feel. . . .

ME: Oh, I can't—I'd feel too shy and funny. . . .

JERRY: If you care about him, and if you hurt him, you must. . . .

ME: I'll write him a letter . . .

JERRY: OK. Do it right now, and I'll take it when I leave for work.

ME: You're *crazy!*

JERRY: Jo—there is only one thing that is unbearable for me, and that is that you shouldn't go on growing and changing, no matter what it costs. . . .

ME: OK. OK.

THE FIRST LETTER

Dear Paul,

I behaved like an idiot yesterday, and I must tell you how sorry I am. What was really happening is that I was discovering how very much I care for you and how sad I was to discover you have been suffering so much pain. It was so dumb of me not to just tell you that, quietly, instead of becoming so efficient and full of advice. After I left you, I felt such a wave of compassion and loving; if that can help, ever, I want it to.

Love,
Jo

I showed the letter to Jerry. He said, "It's all right, but I still think you should call."

ॐ

When I came home from work today, Jerry told me that Paul had called. He left a message with Jerry: "Just tell Jo that I got her wonderfully kind letter, and appreciate it so much."

ॐ

And today a letter:

> My Dearest Jo:
> It is I who should apologize; I should have remembered that you have such a tender heart that my troubles would throw you. I took advantage of your goodness. I had a nice talk with Jerry when I called. He sounds like a fine person. And I don't want to burden you with my problems. I have had them a long time and will manage. But I am warmed—deeply touched—by your concern.
>
> Warmest love,
Paul

⌒⌒

That was how it began. After that, either I was out of town, or Paul was away on vacation. We began writing letters back and forth. His were funny, gay, loving. I began to feel excited, to be preoccupied with thoughts of him— even began having sexual fantasies. That *really* scared me. But I tried to allow my feelings to come, without censorship.

There were things I found I couldn't tell Jerry—things that I felt might hurt him. I began to understand privacy and that it was not at all impossible to love two people at the same time.

One night about three weeks ago, I found myself thinking of Paul when Jerry and I were making love. It was as if God was punishing me for not understanding about Jerry and Nina! I had been so obsessed with images of their being together—that had come between Jerry and myself for such a long time. Now the images were different. I felt so guilty, frightened—ashamed.

Today I went to see Eve for the first time in several

months, told her what had been happening. Her eyes filled with tears when I told her about Jerry's attitude—and then, after my halting, embarrassed confession about the fantasies, the preoccupation with another man, she said, very softly, "Jo, what you are learning is that loving makes more loving, not less. Your thoughts of Paul when you are with Jerry might only add to what you can give Jerry; it is opening yourself to being a woman, loving something universal about men, the need to be there for a man who you love, whoever he may be. One feeling doesn't interfere with the other, it enhances it."

It seems to me that both Eve and Jerry must be crazy and that I am getting myself into a dangerous and possibly disastrous situation. But that doesn't make it go away.

⌒

Paul and I had a lovely lunch together—the longest time we have ever spent with each other. We had a meeting this morning, and when we left, the implication we left with the others was that we had a lot of work to do—which turned out to be a three-hour lunch!

It's almost spring; you can feel the change happening. There are tiny buds on the trees, and the sun feels different. We walked in the park, had lunch at the zoo, watched the children with their boats at the sailboat pond, walked on up to the museum. When we are together, time becomes obsolete, hours seem like seconds; we have so much to say to each other, so much to tell each other about ourselves—so much to learn. I know we are helping each other. Paul has been waiting for years for somone to come along and help him out of the lethargy, the psychological paralysis, that keeps him from escaping from his unhappiness; and for me, there is such joy in feeling loved, not by one but by two men—and what men! I can't understand it at all. They are both handsome and charming and gentle and bright; how could two such men choose *me*? Jerry is right; the more full of joy I feel about myself, the more I love him. I feel so young! I have more energy, I do better work, I feel all of living so intensely. Jerry says he told me so! I tell him when I'm seeing Paul, but I realize that it would be foolish to confide everything to him. He doesn't want me to, and it would be disloyal to Paul. It is a hard balance to find, but there is no lying—just limits to what needs to be said.

Paul has told me that he was not at all unaware of the fact that when we first met, I was unhappy. He tells me my face is about as inscrutable as Charlie Chaplin's! He says that he doubts if he could have allowed himself to begin to feel any loving feelings if there hadn't been the hope that we might both divorce and marry each other. He's so square compared to Jerry. He's just like me! He doesn't understand at all that I can love two people—and he is constantly preoccupied with my life with Jerry.

He says he has never in his life been as close to anyone as he is to me, that he has told me more about himself in a few months than to his wife in all the years of their marriage. He finds this utterly shocking, when I am married to someone else. And there I am, having to experience what I was so absolutely sure was beyond possibility just a couple of years ago.

⤴

How crazy can things get? When I tell Jerry that Paul won't see me if he has to lie to his wife about it, Jerry says, "The poor man is demented! He's *crazy*! He's miserable at home, he loves you—to not even take you to dinner or the theater, when it would give him so much pleasure? Craziness!" Paul, on the other hand, when he heard that Jerry was going away for five or six weeks, was appalled. "Jerry is a weirdo," he said. "My God, to be married to *you*—and to need to go away? Craziness!"

When Jerry and I talked about this irony, Jerry concluded, "Paul and I are both right; he's right that I'm crazy, and I'm right that he's crazy."

⌣⌣

I am going to meet Paul at a meeting and then have dinner with him afterward. Jerry wanted to work late, so I am home alone. I have just finished getting dressed and have come to the conclusion that I have regressed to adolescence. It took me about an hour and a half to decide what to wear; even the decision about which perfume to use was agonizing! This business of experiencing oneself as deeply as possible and allowing all kinds of feelings to surface can really drive one nuts!

And of course I'm ready much too early, sitting here with my heart pounding and my knees shaking. It seems incredible that when I get to the meeting everyone will think that I am mature, successful, middle-aged woman—serious and concerned about the subject to be discussed. I will be the only person there who will know I am a young girl going on a Very Important Date.

⌣⌣

I simply cannot believe what is happening to me. It is utterly fantastic. I try as hard as I can to remember back to two or three years ago—is it really that long?—to how I felt when I found out Jerry was having an affair, and somehow relate that to what has been happening to me, and it seems that there must be two separate people—such disparity couldn't exist in one person—such total change. And yet that is exactly what has happened.

I am totally distracted. Can't work, can't write, can't do anything. Going around in circles. Jerry is kinder and more loving than ever before in our marriage, and I die of guilt that it isn't enough, that my mind wanders away from him as readily as from everything else. I am scared out of my mind. I am terrified to be so vulnerable. And yet, on the other hand, beyond my self-consciousness and concern with being lovable is this terrible need to somehow try to make up to Paul for the miseries of a horrendous marriage.

Whenever we are together, or talking on the phone, it seems that forty conversations get started; none ever gets finished. We never have enough time together; we always feel frustrated, letdown, afterward—and then wildly exhilarated by the next contact. I never imagined it could happen. Part of me is glad, part horrified and in retreat. Part knowing that I have reached a new level of understanding that will be with me no matter what happens—that the unpredictable, the irrational, is so powerful. And that when you give loving free rein, you have to take the consequences. By what accident did this thing happen? Did I have any idea earlier? Did we both dimly perceive it from the beginning?

All day and all night there are images of his face, of conversations, of "scenes" I manufacture; I seem lost in another world more real than anything that is now happening to me. It seems incredible that nobody notices. Or do they? I find myself increasingly impatient and short with everyone; don't want to be bothered, distracted; wish he and I could go away alone for a long time to figure out what to do. I am frightened about the cruise with Jerry. I'm afraid I'll spend the whole two weeks longing to be with Paul. Intolerable! The guilt and fear will overwhelm me, even without the longings.

It seems so unfair to Jerry, and yet if I said I didn't want to go I'd hurt him horribly. We can't get the money back anyway. He says he can take it, no matter what, but I don't think he knows what he is saying.

I feel terribly shy and scared. I want to love so much, and I'm so terrified of it. I am more and more preoccupied with *his* need and my wanting to make *him* happier—and as that happens, I forget my inhibitions and fears. I am violently, wildly in love, and still loving Jerry at the same time. Most of all, wishing I had felt so ready and so free when Jerry and I first met. But you can't go back, make an old relationship new again.

What would I feel if Jerry had an affair again? I can't imagine. I told Paul I ought to find him a wife. He looked me straight in the eye and asked if I really meant it. We skirt the edges—looking love and saying love, but somehow still covertly, and retreating at the moment when the glare of it is there. I can't breathe—both wonder and terror catch my breath.

Even as I realize that Jerry is a giant of a man and that my life is inexorably and forever tied to him, I also understand the reasons for the other love. I have a sense of life passing painfully fast; I have never been in love with anyone else but Jerry, no sexual adventures ever in my whole life; so repressed, that our early time together was nowhere near what it might have been. I guess that's a major part of what is happening—a terrible urgency to experience "young love."

When Paul and I are together, I am pulled forward into great waves of passionate feeling and then left, often for weeks at a time, hanging in uncertainty—sure I imagined the whole thing. And then, when I'm sure it's ridiculous and I am fantasizing the whole thing, there will be a call that makes it all seem real again.

It is mostly painful; the preoccupation bothers me. Jerry's behavior is simply fantastic. Almost too much so! He tells me if I don't do what I need for growing he'll divorce me. His lack of jealousy makes me a little mad, though. There is no pleasing me! I said, "I love you so much I could die." He answers, "Love me enough to love." An unbelievable man. He understands growing and love like no one I have ever known.

It is painful to have reached a point in my development where I think I could really welcome an affair and to find that this is not someone who can accept or settle for what I am prepared to give. Or is that exactly why we chose each other? Because we both knew it would go nowhere, but might just reassure each of us that we are still lovable? All I know is that allowing myself to feel all this, profoundly, changes me forever. I am undefended, open. I can love more easily from now on. What a strange time for this to happen to me! Whatever else may happen, it puts Jerry's experience into a context where I can deal with it, and where the pain is greatly diminished. Maybe that's what I needed most, simply to experience the feeling of loving someone else, to know how one can be exultant and tormented and still in love with one's spouse.

I wonder what will happen. When there is silence, I think I will die, and that I must end the relationship quickly and not let it start up again. And then, when there is contact again, I can't let it go. Such feelings of warmth and excitement and wanting the adventure of it. Most of all I think there is a playfulness between us that I never experienced before. We are alike in some ways—especially in our jokes and laughter. With Jerry there is always an undercurrent of something serious and quiet. This humor is different—earthy and devilish.

If it just stays this way or deteriorates even more, I will still be grateful it happened. I am learning what I am really like. I am a passionate woman! If I were young now, I would not hold myself back from life. One cannot change the past, but it is good and necessary for me to understand what I missed. I hope it will happen now or sometime. I'm ready now. Almost half a century it took! It will be a miracle, but that's easy! The real miracle was the opening to who I am and can be. I'm so full of love and loving. And it isn't going to waste. It's there for Jerry and even for myself *to* myself.

ᕔᗝ

DIALOGUE

ME: Remember a long time ago I asked about Nina's coming to your funeral? And how if it was the other way around, you couldn't love me if you could be grateful toward another man instead of jealous? Well, I think I understand that now. Even though I haven't actually had an affair, loving somebody else and being loved has only made me a happier person. I feel more beautiful, more womanly. I love you more, not less. And it makes sense to me that you could thank Paul for making me feel so beloved, if I were to die.

JERRY: You are so beautiful, my growing girl. That's a wonderful gift—telling me that.

ME: [*laughing*] In fact, to tell you the truth, I can even imagine the scene. I just died suddenly, and you are at the funeral chapel. Everybody is crying—*sobbing!*—and you are inconsolable! Suddenly you see Paul standing at the door. He looks anguished, but is afraid to come in. You go over and throw your arms around him and

you cry together, holding each other. He suddenly
realizes what is happening and looks shocked—and you
say, "I'm so glad she had so much love from both of us."
JERRY: I think that's exactly what would happen. . . .
ME: Darling—if you die first and if Nina comes to your
funeral, I would do the same thing now.
[*This has to be one of the craziest conversations we
have ever had. We both get up from the kitchen table
and hold each other, crying. I think this wonderful man
is getting through to me about the meaning of love.*]

∾

I began to have second thoughts several days after the last
entry: is Jerry really teaching me how to love, or is he, quite
unconsciously perhaps, encouraging me to have an affair so
as to assuage his guilt for having hurt me?
I decided to ask Margaret.
"Nonsense!" she said. "Jerry is *sorry* he hurt you, but you
must remember that he is a man who has suffered very much
in his early years, and has struggled so hard to become more
alive himself. He is not capable of the luxury of minor guilt."
As soon as she said that, I knew she was right. I see it so
clearly in Jerry's eyes when he talks about his wish for me
to be most alive. It's a kind of religious fervor. Listening to
him, watching his expression, I know it is not guilt. I guess
what I feel is that if I ever *do* hurt him or frighten him, it
must not be because I have withdrawn from life; that's the
only kind of pain he couldn't tolerate.

∾

It had been a long, unhappy day; Jerry and I hadn't really
had much time for each other all week. We had dinner to-

gether, and Jerry, who had to go out to an evening meeting, suggested we lie down on the bed together for a few minutes —hold each other, talk quietly—rest.

It was lovely. We talked about whatever important things had been happening to each of us, and just holding each other—the warm body contact—made me feel mellow and relaxed as I hadn't felt all day.

Paul and I had had a silly quarrel at lunch. We were both feeling tense—not enough time to talk, to be together—and he'd withdrawn, and I'd left him abruptly, in a huff. He hadn't called later in the afternoon, although we had some work to discuss; I knew he was leaving for Chicago the next morning. All I said to Jerry was that it had been a difficult and irritating day. He was warm and loving, and I began to feel at peace—cherished.

The telephone rang. I rolled over to answer it. Paul, in a telephone booth at the airport. "I'm leaving. I love you. I'll be back in a week. Don't go away." His voice so sad—I can see the tired, drawn expression on his face. I sit up, holding the phone, my back to Jerry. The close intimate mood with him is shattered; I feel uneasy, shy—embarrassed. Jerry knows immediately who is on the phone and gets up and leaves the room to dress for his meeting. Paul needs some reassurance, some comforting, before he leaves. He's worried about his kids; he's worried about his job; it's just too much if he is also worried about me.

Jerry comes in, ready to leave, waves good-bye and is gone. I feel frightened. What a crazy, unbelievable situation! It is incredible.

Waves of loving. First for Paul, who *did* call, then for Jerry, who allows this, who was holding me and who *will come back*, in spite of the untimely interruption.

I call the place where Jerry's meeting is to take place and leave a message; would they please ask my husband to call his home when he gets there? A few minutes later Jerry calls, but I hear traffic noises in the background. He hasn't gotten to the meeting yet and hasn't gotten my message; he is calling on his own from a phone booth because he knew I'd feel worried and guilty!

"That was really crazy," I said. "I felt so close to you, so happy, and then to be interrupted that way—I thought maybe you'd be angry or jealous." Not at all, my remarkable, unbelievable husband tells me. He admires Paul—liked him immediately when he first met him and is filled with compassion for his plight. "I called because I knew *you* would be upset," he says, "and I wanted to reassure you. I knew Paul was going away, and I'm glad he called to say good-bye to you."

I feel such an overwhelming love for this man who is allowing my life to happen so fully. "How can I ever tell you how much I love you?" I ask. "By being all you need to be," he tells me again. All I know is that when he says this my love for him becomes deeper and stronger. I feel joyful and whole. I feel more alive and more womanly than I have ever felt before.

I am asleep when Jerry comes home, but awaken when I hear him getting into bed. I remember his leaving and what he said on the phone. What a man! I roll over, close, cling to him, want to make love to him. No one in all the world has ever loved me so unconditionally—been so completely for me. It is true that the permission to live fully only increases one's capacity to love. Our lovemaking on this night is ecstatic—beyond this immediate time and place. I feel as if in some way we fill the universe, that in this profound kind of loving one draws on all one's life and all one's feelings—

that there is nothing bad or wrong about also thinking of Paul—of all loved men and women in one's life—that this kind of touching, moving together, beyond self, is the ultimate in being human and in loving, and that everything I am and that Jerry is can be part of where we are together. For the first time I find I can even allow Nina into this moment. Jerry has taught me what loving is really all about.

ᘉ

Paul and I have been having a terrible time. I can't stop fighting with him—responding to everything he says or does in a bitchy way. I scream and yell—and then hate myself, feel flooded by guilt and remorse. After a particularly unpleasant conversation, I wrote him a letter asking him to leave me alone—stop calling me for a while, until I could decide whether or not I wanted to cool it.

Paul called as soon as he got the letter. In a withering tone of voice, he just said, "Don't be ridiculous!" It was unexpected—the one reaction I guess I hadn't thought of, and I couldn't help myself—I laughed. But he didn't let me off that easy. In a cold and angry voice he said, "Let me ask you something. Is there anything more you feel I could be doing? I'm spending a hundred dollars a week on psychotherapy; I am trying to change a lifetime of self-destructive behavior; I am trying to face a depression that has been going on for most of my adulthood; I am trying to change my relationship to work, wife, children; I am even trying desperately to *feel*, for the first time in my life. Just what more do you want me to do?"

I like the anger—the authority—the end of what used to be a passive, awed respect from a distance. This sounds like somebody who might begin to really love!

ᘉ

Sometimes—what am I saying?—*most* of the time!—I wonder why Jerry and I don't do what most of our contemporaries seem to do—settle for where we are, rest on our laurels, stop this nonsense about always searching for being more than we are at any given time. It is so exhausting!

We both have dreadful colds right now; we are both convinced that we got sick because we wanted to avoid facing some new or old feelings. We have had too much company, tried to meet too many other people's demands. Then anger and fatigue set in, and we are off and running (at the nose!).

In addition to too many chores and too much socializing, I find that I am utterly exhausted by my vulnerability—the degree to which I allow myself to risk in loving—and then get shot down, feel rejected, unloved. Now, looking back, the pain of Jerry's affair seems less monumental than what I am experiencing in relation to Paul. Of course, part of this is the remarkable human talent for forgetting pain.

I paced up and down all day today, couldn't settle down to work, felt exhausted with my cold but couldn't nap. I felt too lousy to go out, but knew I needed to see Eve. I hate bothering her on the phone—especially at the end of the day when I know she needs to relax. However, by seven P.M. I couldn't control the impulse to at least hear her reassuring voice. When she answered the phone and I asked if she was busy, she said, munching happily into the phone, "I'm eating a delicious steak." I started to apologize for calling. "I hate taking advantage of you, and I tried to leave you alone today, and I don't want to interfere with your dinner, and I can call back tomorrow morning. . . ."

At which point Eve, still chewing, said, "SHUT UP—and start talking!"

It was a great line and very funny—but it also says a lot about why Eve has been a source of such comfort, inspiration, mothering—most of all, demanding the best of me. She knows just when to shut off the irrelevancies, the rationalizations, the time-wasting apologies, and get me back into the work of growing. Sometimes I wonder if I could have lived through these last few years without her. Not well! She assures me that I am "fantastic material" to work with—and at last I know she is right! But there is a combination of tender-toughness about her, as well as a staggering brilliance of insightfulness that make my adventures in living purposeful, profoundly moving, and deeply significant. It seems to me that everyone ought to have such a teacher. We need to find ways to do it for each other. As I listen to my friends talk about themselves, I am more and more convinced that no one can ever be objective enough about him or herself; we need a sounding board, the mirror of someone else's mind. What a precious gift Eve has been.

༄

Paul and I have come to a parting of the ways. He is too unhappy about my being married to somebody else! He is also too preoccupied with fighting for his own life.

He tells me about his fantasies when we first met—when he thought I might be as unhappy as he was. He says, "There was a feeling of possession." I try to explain that nobody belongs to anybody except themselves, and he interrupts and says, "You have helped me to think I deserve the best in life; is the little you can spare enough?"

There is no argument. I want him to have the whole of love. But must it be right away? Couldn't it be me for a little while? Even as I ask myself that, I know I am inviting great pain for both of us ultimately. The truth is that underneath all our words is the fact that Paul feels exactly the way I used to feel; he cannot understand how it is possible to love two people at the same time. We look across the table at each other, helpless, hopeless, sad. I think back to where I have been these past few years. Paul is *me*; every word he says made perfect sense to me less than five years ago! It is as if I am talking to myself. It is terrible, but also in a strange way very meaningful and valuable. It sharpens my perception of what has happened to me. To argue with one's own disgarded attitudes is to see more clearly how far one has come.

And then, suddenly, I realize a miracle. What has happened to me can happen to Paul, too! I needed time for growing; so does he. Anything is still possible. And whether he eventually reaches toward me or finds a woman he can love and marry, I cannot deny that we have been good for each other. I know how well I can love, and he knows how lovable he is and that he must never stop learning how to live.

༄

I suddenly realize how addicted I have become to writing; it crosses my mind that it is possible that sometime in the future I may still need to buy a new collection of notebooks —for a book entitled, "Her Affair!"

I got such a beautiful letter from Evelyn today; it sort of put everything into perspective: "I wish you more and more of life's fullness even if you stay in your own garden."

༄

I have been in a rage—feeling uttery helpless, caught— furious because I cannot manipulate, control, what has happened to me.

And then the tears come, torrents. The loss is so great— and it does not help at all to try to cover it up with anger. There is just this terrible, terrible pain—and if I have learned anything, it is that I must endure the anguish—let it happen —live it—and grow through it.

I once thought that nothing could ever make me as unhappy as I was when I found out about Jerry's affair. I realize, with some sense of shock, that I have been crying just as much since falling in love with Paul. Weeping for the ambiguity of my feelings; weeping for his passive acceptance of a life of woes—his inability to take what limited joy is offered; weeping for the "more" each of us can't give the other.

Again those feelings are here, not wanting to live, grieving. So deeply. The only thing that is different is the source of my feelings of rejection. Now it is Paul; I miss him desperately—run to the phone every time it rings—feeling desolate when it's not him, and also relieved because I just can't go on, start all the misery all over again.

I have this feeling that I mustn't burden Jerry with my loss. He knows, of course, that Paul and I agreed not to see each other for a while, and I know he is genuinely sorry for my pain. But I try to do my sobbing when he's not around. Crazy as it sounds, it would be easier for me to tell him I was having an affair than to tell him I am suffering because I am not! I suppose it is because of what Margaret said to me about the only thing Jerry cannot bear is suffering because one is not fully alive

The moments come when I think I cannot stand that burden—of feeling everything so much—one more second. Why can't I turn into a nice, quiet, normal sort of person, settling for a life that is closer to the surface of one's existence? It's a dumb question; I can't. Most of living, most of being human, is tragic in some way. Better to live it and feel it and thereby gain a few moments, now and then, of piercing joy, rather than run away from all of it.

⌒つ

DIALOGUE

EVE: You look so beautiful today. . . .

ME: You're *crazy!* I came here today to tell you how depressed I am. I look terrible.

EVE: Well, let's talk about it. There is a softness and a radiance. . . .

ME: I think you need to see a shrink; your judgment is failing.

EVE: You must be getting better if you have figured *that* out!

ME: Enough with the humor. I just figured everything out, in the taxi coming here. My problem is that I get impatient. I always make an appointment with you too soon. If I'd wait another day or two I would figure out what's wrong without you.

EVE: Would you consider the possibility that these insights come *because* you've made an appointment?

ME: You are getting too predictable; that is the answer I assigned to you in the cab. . . . Anyway, I think I've been very depressed for quite a while—maybe the whole six weeks I've been dragging around with this cold. Last night I was very sad and I couldn't cry. I am willing to concede this may have something to do with my sinus condition.

EVE: What happened?

ME: Paul, naturally. But loving and not being loved back is only part of it. I thought I was ready to be brave and free. But it was self-delusion. I'm a fraud. I picked someone who was safe, who would never ask me for what I thought I was ready to offer. I'd pretend I was ready, but I'd be safe. I haven't really grown or changed at all. . . .

EVE: Darling, stop beating yourself on the head. You and

Paul are such complicated people; don't oversimplify. You could not have predicted his behavior any more than he could. And don't you realize—you *have* had a love affair with him—the rest is technicalities. He loves you, but he is not as brave as you are. You have given him so much, so freely—ah, now I know why you look the way you do! It's the softness, it's letting all the pain in. . . .

ME: OK, so I'll cry. My God, how it *hurts*! I feel as if someone is shooting me with poison arrows. I can't bear to feel so much.

EVE: But you have never really run away from pain. I don't know anyone who has gone on growing and discovering and sensitizing herself as you have. It's a radiance all around you—you are a beautiful human being. Whatever happens, you are alive and full of love and warm the lives of everyone around you. . . .

ME: Do I have to pay extra when *you* cry?

EVE: Oh, shut up.

⌒

When I was in high school, everyone thought I would become a writer. I never did. There were so many other interests and occupations that took priority. Keeping this diary has brought me back to that earlier self. I thought at first that what I was doing was simply giving myself someplace to go to scream—on paper in a lined notebook.

It has turned out to be so much more than that. It has become a homecoming—back to a self I have neglected. I find that I want to go on writing in my notebook, beyond the handling of pain. It has become an essential of my life. I wake up in the morning eager to make some new notes, and as the days go by, I find my perceptions sharpened—there seem to be so many events that take on special importance and need to be recorded. I observe my life and myself with a new awareness, a greater sensitivity.

I suspect that for myself the most important event of these last years has been my writing. A new beginning of an un-lived part of myself that exploded into life at a time of great stress. I think I learned the difference between empty pain and creative pain, without even realizing how lucky I was!

I suppose what has changed the most is what I *do* about feelings of frustration, how I live it. I experience my life more deeply; I have no rules or formulas to live by any more; I make no claims on myself or anyone else to make life easy or comfortable. What I seemed to have gained most of all is in my capacity to love and to be loved far more pro-foundly than ever before. And most of all I have discovered a quiet inner river in myself—a flow from my deepest being into words on paper. It is the last gift I expected from this adventure. I look ahead with neither dread nor joy; only with wonder at where I have been and curiosity about what lies ahead.

This morning Paul called. We haven't spoken to each other for, roughly speaking, about six weeks, four days, and fifteen minutes! At the sound of his voice, that comfortable tranquillity I had been enjoying for a few days vanished.

"Hi," he said cheerily. "This is your friendly neighbor-hood masochist calling. You may not remember the name, but I hope you remember the voice—the anguished cry for help."

"Thank God," was all I could seem to say.

It seems that the two of us have been invited to address

a Very Important Meeting at a three-day conference in another city.

"I'd like you to give some serious thought to attending,"
Paul said. "And I hope you will use your creative imagination in making your decision." Paul is always funny when
what we are saying to each other is most deadly serious.

I *am* giving it serious consideration. If my legs stop
trembling, and if I can catch my breath, I may go out and
buy myself a new notebook.

Jerry and I are sitting on the beach, mesmerized by the
sound of the waves. This has always been one of our most
necessary forms of nourishment—that sound. He is lying
back on a beach chair looking at the ocean. There is a far-
away look in his eyes, and I know this means he is con-
templating some abstraction, some new hypothesis in his
work. Soon he will casually inform me of some new idea. He
looks wonderful. There is a relaxed craggyness about him, and
he gets handsomer as he gets older. His beautiful, wavy,
abundant gray hair blows in the breeze. He has become
more and more charismatic—I see it when I hear him give
a speech. Both men and women love him. In the past few
years I have become so much more sensitized to how many
women fall in love with him. It now seems absolutely fantastic that he continues to choose me above all others.
Fantastic in the sense of wonderful—not surprising. How
marvelous it is, at long last, to know I'm worth it!

It seems to me now that we are indestructible, that we
love each other in a way that becomes *more* powerful the
less we cling to each other. I cannot believe, it but I know
it is true. It is as if we are one tree—a venerable maple that
turns that ecstatic red-yellow-orange-pink every fall, and

only becomes more beautiful the richer and older it gets, with more and more branches going off in all directions. The branches are separate, have no immediate contact with each other, are often far apart—but they share the trunk and are indivisible from it. How glorious to have come to this understanding in the fall of our lives, when the vivid colors scream exultantly. I find myself shocked by the next thought: the more new branches each of us has, the richer the foliage —and I want more for both of us—whether it be love or work or travel or whatever adventures lie ahead. We may weep when winter comes—but hopefully without regret for opportunities lost.

There is no question that there are times when I wish my life had been more serene. I know a few couples who actually have never gone through the kind of upheaval we have experienced. For a moment here or there I think to myself that it must be wonderful to be comfortably satisfied with only one partner all of one's life. But if you are going to have a passionate love affair with life, if you thrive on divine discontent, well, then, folks, there is nothing to do but hold on for dear life and take the consequences!

The sound of the surf seems to break my heart. I feel sad and alive; there is somehow a mixture of joyful wonder and restless foreboding in this mysterious, powerful sea before me. I know Jerry and I are resting only briefly. Neither of us knows what is in store for us, separately or together. We only know we must allow all of life to happen to us, holding nothing back. It is terrifying and wonderful. We are the brave.